# LEONARD

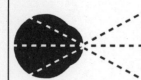

This Large Print Book carries the
Seal of Approval of N.A.V.H.

# LEONARD

## MY FIFTY-YEAR FRIENDSHIP
## WITH A REMARKABLE MAN

---

# WILLIAM SHATNER
# WITH DAVID FISHER

**THORNDIKE PRESS**
*A part of Gale, Cengage Learning*

GALE
CENGAGE Learning·

Farmington Hills, Mich • San Francisco • New York • Waterville, Maine
Meriden, Conn • Mason, Ohio • Chicago

GALE
CENGAGE Learning®

Copyright © 2016 by William Shatner.
Thorndike Press, a part of Gale, Cengage Learning.

**ALL RIGHTS RESERVED**
Thorndike Press® Large Print Biographies and Memoirs.
The text of this Large Print edition is unabridged.
Other aspects of the book may vary from the original edition.
Set in 16 pt. Plantin.

### LIBRARY OF CONGRESS CATALOGING-IN-PUBLICATION DATA

Names: Shatner, William, author. | Fisher, David, 1946- author.
Title: Leonard : my fifty-year friendship with a remarkable man / William Shatner
    with David Fisher.
Description: Large print edition. | Waterville, Maine : Thorndike Press Large Print,
    2016. | © 2016 | Series: Thorndike Press large print biographies and memoirs
Identifiers: LCCN 2016000432 | ISBN 9781410487438 (hardback) | ISBN 1410487431
    (hardcover)
Subjects: LCSH: Nimoy, Leonard—Friends and associates. | Shatner,
    William—Friends and associates. | Actors—United States—Biography. | Large
    type books. | BISAC: BIOGRAPHY & AUTOBIOGRAPHY / Entertainment &
    Performing Arts.
Classification: LCC PN2287.N55 S53 2016b | DDC 791.4502/8092—dc23
LC record available at http://lccn.loc.gov/2016000432

Published in 2016 by arrangement with St. Martin's Press, LLC

Printed in Mexico
1 2 3 4 5 6 7 20 19 18 17 16

I am dedicating this book to a human being who lived his life for over eighty-three years, whose journey was filled with joy and anger, cynicism and idealism, the endless array of emotions that constantly change and evolve. We humans go through life barnacled with the detritus of life — it's a drag, causing change, what once was passion changes to indifference — joy becomes sorrow and love has many hues. All the interweaving elements of human existence. Thus, I am that, you are that, and he was that. I dedicate this book to my dear friend Leonard Nimoy and his loving family.

# ONE

Death ends a life, but it does not
end a relationship.
— PLAYWRIGHT ROBERT ANDERSON

At the conclusion of the second Star Trek movie, *The Wrath of Khan,* the *Enterprise* is facing destruction. The starship had less than four minutes to escape the activation of the Genesis Device, which will reorganize all matter. But it can't get away fast enough because the warp drive has been damaged. It can be repaired — but it's a suicide mission. Enough radiation has leaked into the reactor room to kill anyone going in there to make those repairs. As Dr. McCoy tells Spock, "No human can tolerate the radiation that's in there."

To which Spock responds, ever logically, "But as you are so fond of observing, Doctor, I am not human." After incapacitating McCoy with a Vulcan nerve pinch, Spock

7

goes into the reactor room and saves the ship and its crew. But the cost is his own life.

When Kirk realizes what has happened, he runs down to the engine room. Spock is still barely alive. The two men, who have fought together throughout the universe, are separated by a clear plate glass wall. In his last moments, Spock tells Kirk, "Don't grieve, Admiral . . . it is logical. The needs of the many . . . outweigh . . ."

"— the needs of the few," Kirk finishes.

"Or the one," Spock adds, then places the palm of his hand, open with Vulcan salute, on the glass. On the other side, Kirk lays his hand on the wall, their hands seemingly touching. A final good-bye. With his dying breath, Spock tells Kirk, "I have been . . . and always shall be . . . your friend. Live long . . . and prosper."

At the conclusion of the 2001 documentary *Mind Meld: Secrets Behind the Voyage of a Lifetime,* which is simply a long conversation between Leonard Nimoy and me about our lifelong journey to places no man had gone before, we are together in his den. Earlier in this film, we were looking at a framed photograph of us in our *Star Trek* costumes on the cover of *TV Guide.* "This is us," he'd mused. "Siamese twins."

I agreed, "Yes, you and I. Joined at the hip." A few seconds later, I added, "You and I have spent more than half our lives together. I think of you as one of my dearest friends, my dearest. And I truly love, I love you."

Leonard wasn't a man given to public displays of emotion. Much like the character Spock, he was very reserved. "The same," was the best response he could muster at that moment. But at the very end of the documentary, as we stood next to each other looking into the camera, he suddenly and quite unexpectedly threw his arm around my shoulders and blurted, "You're my best friend."

In life, as well as through the characters we created on *Star Trek,* Mr. Spock and Captain James T. Kirk, Leonard Nimoy was my best friend. And like the millions of people who loved him, I will miss him forever.

Leonard and I were born four days apart. While I was born first, and was therefore the wiser, more mature, and more experienced one, he simply enjoyed pointing out, "You're a lot older than I am." Although neither one of us remembered it, we met briefly for the first time in 1964 when we both appeared in an episode of *The Man from U.N.C.L.E.* I played a supposedly drunken bon vivant; he was the Russian bad guy. In our first scene together, I slung my arm over Leonard's shoulder, raised my martini glass, and muttered, "Calvin Coolidge! How are you, Cal baby? Want a taste of this?" But our friendship, our friendship that was to last fifty years, actually began in July 1965, when we filmed our first *Star Trek* episode together.

Obviously, neither one of us could have imagined that eventually we would become best friends. Nor did we have the slightest hint that we were creating two of the most iconic characters in American cultural history. We were two working actors showing up to do the job. Honestly, until Leonard and I developed our relationship — with the exception of my wives — I never had a real friend; I didn't even know what a friend was. I had never had anyone in my life to whom I could completely emotionally unburden myself. There certainly have been some wonderful people I have been close to, people I know I could rely on, but as far as speaking openly and revealing that which is most troublesome and most secretive, secure in the knowledge it will remain as buried in their breasts as it is in mine, there was only Leonard. We worked together for three seasons. During production, actors will spend more time with each other than with their families. When actors work together for a lengthy period of time, comfortable friendships often develop. We've worked together under great stress and forged a common bond. We've faced ridicule and shared feelings of inadequacy. We've pushed each other past exhaustion to try to do better work. We've fought the front office and the business staff, and we've made something good. Through it all, many of us come to love and depend on each other.

Before doing *Star Trek,* for example, I did a series called *For the People* with Howard Da Silva, Lonny Chapman, and Jessica Walter. It was a wonderful show, and they were all my best friends. When it ended, we hugged and told each other how much we loved each other and pledged eternal friendship and never saw each other again. Long after *Star Trek,* I did *Boston Legal* with James Spader. My God, I love James Spader. We cared for each other, we respected each other, and I learned from James Spader the value of facing a problem rather than burying it and hoping it goes away. The characters we played were so close I suggested we marry, so as my senility took control, he would have legal authority to take care of

11

me. Off the set, we weren't quite that close, but certainly I consider him a very good friend. If I called him and asked the wildest favor, I have no doubt he would respond. When the series ended, we knew we would be friends forever. And with very few exceptions, we have never spoken since.

Actors' friendships are like that. They tend to be deep and temporary. During the closing party, we hold each other firmly, intimately; man, woman, and child, we've been through the wars together. I love you. I'll never forget you. You're my friend forever. But within a few days, if you're lucky, you've got another job, and your life is filled with all new and equally wonderful people, and you never see each other again. Every series, every movie or play I've done, they were all my good friends, and I never saw them again.

But with Leonard, it was different. What should have happened was that after three years of making a mildly successful series and gaining a great deal of respect and good feeling toward each other, after our last day on the set, we each should have gone in whatever direction our careers took us. But this was a unique situation; there never has been anything comparable. Rather than being forgotten in television history, after going into syndication, *Star Trek* grew to become one of the most popular programs in history. It became part of the American dialogue. Leonard and I made five movies together; he directed two of them, and I directed one. We attended several conventions a year and otherwise made appearances and even commercials. While circumstances should have taken us to different places, the unprecedented success of *Star Trek* continually brought us together.

Our friendship took root in the many common bonds we shared. We had similar childhoods; both of us were raised in lower-middle-class Orthodox Jewish immigrant families, we grew up in religiously mixed neighborhoods in great cities, and both of us found the magic of acting when we were very young and filled our emotional needs with it. We both defied our fathers to pursue our dreams. We had our families, our children, our homes and marriages; we both had a strong work ethic, a need for approval, and a great respect for the craft we'd chosen. We went through marriages and painful divorces together, we fought the studio together, we even got tinnitus together. Mostly, though, we shared an extraordinary experience that very few people have ever known. We were carried and buffeted by the same winds, and there truly was no one else who could understand what that meant. But beyond all that, beyond the success and the recognition and the applause, I really liked being with the guy. Leonard was smart and funny and nice; he had learned from all the challenges in his life and gotten through them and taken from them a great deal of wisdom that he was kind enough to share with me.

My respect for him was profound. I was in awe of his creative talents. There are people who rush through life pursuing various passions; Leonard's life unfolded slowly, revealing passions I wouldn't have guessed were there. As an actor, he created an archetype character that has become part of our culture. He was a very successful director, a wonderful fine-arts photographer; he wrote and starred in plays and published books of his poetry. Leonard Nimoy was the only man I have ever known who could perform Shakespeare in Yiddish; he could make you appreciate the beauty even if you didn't understand a word beyond, "*Oy gevalt,* Hamlet."

He was my friend. But according to the Global Family Reunion project, we also were distantly related; supposedly I am Leonard's wife Susan's fifth cousin twice

14

removed's wife's aunt's husband's uncle's wife's second grandnephew. Admittedly, that was not something we ever discussed, but in fact, on some level, we were related; we came from the same tribe. Leonard and I were both products of the same history. Our lives were shaped by the same historical hatreds and the courage and desire of our families — Jews who fled eastern Europe to escape persecution. Leonard's mother and father came from the village of Iziaslav in Ukraine. His mother and grandmother were smuggled out of the brand-new Soviet Union hidden under bales of hay in the back of a wagon and made it to America; his father snuck across the border on foot, sailing first to Buenos Aires and then on to New York. When his father found out that a cousin in Boston was opening a barbershop, he settled there, remet Leonard's mother, and married her. Like Leonard, my family also came here from eastern Europe; my grandparents were from Ukraine, Lithuania, and the Austro-Hungarian Empire. Leonard and I were both born in March 1931.

Both of us grew up in the west end: my family lived in the west end of Montreal; his family lived in the Boston neighborhood known as the West End. My father was in the *schmatta* business, manufacturing inexpensive suits for the workingman who owned only that one suit. Leonard's father had the local barbershop. I grew up in a mostly Catholic neighborhood, while Boston's West End was the American melting pot, Italians and Jews and Poles and Irish, everybody who came from Europe, and even as Leonard described it, "A sprinkling of blacks." In most immigrant communities, there was a great sense of equality; we all had nothing together. I can remember the pushcarts and the beggars, the ice man delivering hunks of ice to keep the small icebox cold, the singsong and the bells of the merchants as they drove slowly down the street. Leonard could recite the merchant's singsongs, singing out in Yiddish, "We have threads, we have needles, we have cloth, we have ribbons. What do you need? It's all here on my cart."

While neither one of us actually came from poverty, growing up in the Depression, we both saw too much of it. Leonard always remembered the families who had been evicted from their apartment, sitting on the sidewalk with all their belongings, waiting for someone to come with a wagon and take them somewhere else, never to be heard from in the old neighborhood again.

16

I'm not sure why, but in retrospect, I actually knew quite a bit more about Leonard's childhood than he knew about mine. Leonard was a wonderful storyteller, and he would weave these vivid word portraits of the people and places of his childhood. His father's barbershop — haircuts twenty-five cents, shaves a dime — had three chairs, quite extravagant for that neighborhood, but a lot of life took place in the back room. Apparently, that was the local hangout. There was always a pinochle game going on, maybe some other gambling that nobody talked much about, and if someone was hard up and needed to borrow a few bucks, that was the place to go. Leonard's father was the treasurer of the Iziaslav Letter Society Credit Union, an organization the immigrants all chipped into to offer assistance when it was needed. Leonard remembers people coming into the Modern Barbershop, as it was named, once a week to give his father as much as a dollar.

Leonard and his older brother grew up in an apartment with their parents and grandparents. Like mine, it was a kosher home; maybe we didn't have any luxuries, but we always had three sets of dishes. A lot of Jewish immigrants in the West End, including his grandparents, spoke mostly Yiddish, so

Leonard actually became quite fluent in Yiddish. Leonard loved the sound of that language; he used to repeat some of the wonderful expressions his grandmother used: "You should grow up like an onion, with your head in the ground and your feet in the air." "Go bang your head against the wall when you say you're bored and got nothing to do." By the time we became friends, he was concerned he was losing his facility for the language, so he actually found a Yiddish-speaking psychiatrist in Los Angeles and paid her hourly fee once a week just to sit and speak with him in Yiddish.

He was always proud to be a West Ender. He named his house in Lake Tahoe West End, and that also was the name painted on the back of his boat. People like us, who grew up in that kind of environment, carried the values we learned there with us wherever we went for the rest of our lives. For Leonard, that meant being a responsible citizen; respect other people, give back to the community by helping those people who needed help, work hard, and take responsibility for your actions.

Leonard described his parents as hardworking, extremely ethical, and constantly concerned about what might happen next. "Everything my parents did was colored by fear," he said. " 'What could happen if you did this or did that? So, be safe, just be safe.' " In his family it was his grandfather Sam Spinner who was the real character. When his parents were telling him, "No, don't do it, it's not safe," his grandfather was slipping him a dollar and telling him, "Here, go do something."

It was his grandfather who continually pushed Leonard to go ahead, try it, do it. He was the adventurer in the family, the one who came to America first and then started bringing over the rest of his family one by one. It was my father, Joseph Shatner, who did the same thing for my family: he came here alone at fourteen and slowly and over many years helped bring each of his ten brothers and sisters to America.

My father cut fabric and made suits; Sam Spinner was a leather cutter. I remember Leonard telling me that when he went home after his first few years in Hollywood, his grandfather would reach down and feel the leather on his shoes to determine how well he was doing. If Leonard needed heels, his grandfather knew he wasn't doing well.

And, quite naturally at that time, both of us were exposed to anti-Semitism. I actually had to plan my strategy for getting to my Hebrew school; I'd walk past it on the far

19

side of the street — then race across the street and inside. But I still got in my share of fights with the Catholic kids. I was a tough kid; that was my nickname — "Toughie." Leonard's family called him *liebe,* which was the German word for love. The moment that had the most lasting impression on him took place one day during World War II when his father suddenly laid down his newspaper and said softly, "They're killing Jews." Killing Jews meant the Jews of Europe, in many cases our distant family members. There was a real feeling among all the Jews: that could have been me. For kids the age of Leonard and me, that had a strong impact. There also were a lot of whispered conversations in Jewish homes about whether or not Franklin Roosevelt was good for the Jews. He received a lot of criticism in the Jewish community for not bombing the rail lines to the concentration camps; although some people explained that if he did that, there would be complaints that he was more worried about Jews than the war effort. But what it came down to was that Jews were on their own, they were different, and I suspect Leonard felt that at least as much as I did. It was part of our shared heritage.

And both Leonard and I got called all the

nasty anti-Semitic names. Experiences like that create a sort of subtext, and as we got to know each other, those common experiences helped bind us together. It's almost an emotional shorthand.

We also learned the value of a dollar and inherited a work ethic. Later in life, Leonard would do a very funny impression of me in which he made fun of the fact that I can't stop working. "It's quarter of four," he'd say in his best Shatner. "What's scheduled for four ten? If I'm done here by four thirty-two, can we book something at four forty?" But the reality was that for most of his life, Leonard really never slowed down too much either. It just was in our blood to be anxious about the next job, the next paycheck. In some fashion, we both worked all our lives.

Growing up, I worked as a suit packer in my father's factory; I take great pride in my ability to fold. I've often said if the acting thing hadn't worked out, I would have had a fine career in professional folding.

As a kid, Leonard took any job he could find. He sold newspapers, he worked in his cousin's card shop, he shined shoes, he set up chairs for the Boston Pops. Whatever somebody was paying to be done, he would do it. He even sold vacuums for the Ace

Vacuum Company. The money made a big difference in the family finances. Leonard's biggest memory about the day the Japanese attacked Pearl Harbor, for example, was the fact that he sold all his copies of *The Boston Record* and couldn't get any more of them.

Neither one of us were especially good students. With so much out in the real world to learn, school just didn't hold our attention. But there was one skill at which both of us excelled: we could talk. My mother was an elocution teacher and never hesitated to correct my speech; Leonard once won a declamation contest at the neighborhood settlement house, the Elizabeth Peabody House, by memorizing and reciting the entire text of Longfellow's *The Song of Hiawatha*. If I close my eyes, I can hear his deep and somber voice, playing with Longfellow's words as he says with utter conviction:

By the shore of Gitche Gumee,
By the shining Big-Sea-Water,
At the doorway of his wigwam
In the pleasant Summer morning . . .

And when I do that, it's almost impossible not to smile.

It is, however, a little more difficult but

considerably more fun to imagine the taciturn Mr. Spock reading that poem with both curiosity and a complete lack of emotion.

# Two

It was in our neighborhoods that both of us took our first steps into the future. Acting is such an odd profession. It's a profession in which you spend your life trying to convince people you are someone else. There isn't any single reason young people become actors. Obviously, it can be a lot of fun and play, but I think for most people who take it seriously, it fulfills some type of need. John de Lancie, who created the character Q for several *Star Trek* generations and worked closely with Leonard doing staged readings of great plays, explained he became an actor because "it was the first time in my life that anyone had responded well to anything that I'd done. I grabbed onto it like a life preserver. It gave me an identity."

My mother enrolled me in the Dorothy Davis School for Actors when I was about eight years old. We met in somebody's basement. My mother was a frustrated actress.

She would act out monologues at home for an audience of me. But I suspect she thought it would be a good activity for me; I didn't have any close friends. I suspect it hurt her to see me walking to school each morning all by myself.

Like me, Leonard found acting when he was eight years old. The settlement house was the center of most immigrant neighborhoods. As Leonard described it when he gave the 2012 commencement address at Boston University, "It was a community settlement house which was created to help immigrants find their way into the culture. They offered classes in language, cooking, shopping, kitchen sanitation, dental care and how to apply for a job. There was a gym and a sports program. And there was a small gem of a theater." It was the place to hang out and learn how to be American. Immigrant families had neither the time nor money to spend on culture.

In Leonard's apartment, for example, there were no books. His family had a radio and an old record player and three or four Yiddish records. They would play the same record, a collection of songs sung by Yiddish theater star Seymour Rexite, over and over and over. The Elizabeth Peabody House had a 375-seat theater in which they presented programs for both adults and children. Leonard actually had a pleasant singing voice; he used to sing in his synagogue choir. In fact, his singing at his own bar mitzvah was so good that he was asked to perform the whole ceremony again a week later at another shul. He is still the only man I know whose voice was two bar mitzvahs good! Who else made a guest appearance at a bar mitvah?

Apparently, one afternoon when he was hanging out at the settlement house, they were casting a children's show. They brought him into a music room where a woman was sitting at a piano and asked him to sing. While he never remembered what song he sang, it was enough to earn him a leading role in a production of *Hansel and Gretel.*

Acting came easily to him. It was playing. He could memorize lines, he could sing, and he enjoyed performing. In those days, there were numerous local radio shows for children, and both of us worked on some of those programs. While I was performing heroic acts on *Saturday Morning Fairy Tales,* Leonard was doing Bible stories. Obviously, there was something symbolic about that. Many years later as Captain Kirk, I would be busy rescuing civilizations in distress on distant planets while Leonard's Mr. Spock would be examining the morality of man- and alienkind.

In the pursuit of most professions, there is some sort of loosely defined career path. There are educational requirements that have to be fulfilled or mechanical skills that have to be mastered or an apprentice program that has to be completed. There is no path leading to an acting career; no right way or wrong way, no tests to pass. Talent matters, of course, but it is not enough. I have known many wonderfully talented people who just never got the right opportunity. Often, it is simply a matter of being in the right place at the right time and having some often undefined quality or desirable look; in many situations, it's as much marketability as acting ability. But every actor needs that first break. For Leonard, it was meeting Boris Sagal.

Sagal also had come from Ukraine. He was a Harvard law student with an interest in theater. The settlement house, which was only a ten-cent MTA ride across the Charles River from Harvard, let him stay in one of its guest rooms in exchange for directing plays. He was casting a production of the Clifford Odets play *Awake and Sing!* and put seventeen-year-old Leonard in a leading role. That was the first adult play Leonard

27

had ever done, and it fit him perfectly. It was the story of three generations of a lower-middle-class immigrant Jewish family living together in an apartment in the Bronx. Leonard's character, Ralph Berger, is an idealistic young man who rejects materialism but needs money to buy his own freedom. When I interviewed Leonard on my TV show *Raw Nerve,* he told me about the impact that play had on his life.

"I thought, this is really interesting. This is about people like me . . . It's about our lives and the pressures and the loves and the hates and the angers and the frustrations, the fears.

"This kid I'm playing has the same concerns that I've got: what am I supposed to do with my life and who am I supposed to be . . . The show closes, and I go to the theater to pick up my wardrobe, the clothes that I was wearing in the play. They were my own clothes. The theater was four or five blocks away from my home in Boston. I pick them up, and I'm walking home through the streets of Boston . . . and I realized I was going in the wrong direction. I'm saying to myself, I'm more comfortable there than I am at home. I want to do what's there in the theater. I don't want to do what's happening in that house. There's nothing for me there. I've got to get out of there. That's when I realized I've got to get away."

That job also changed Boris Sagal's life; he forgot about studying law and was accepted at Yale School of Drama and eventually became a successful TV and movie director — and would work with Leonard again.

Coincidently, I was just about the same age as Leonard when I got one of the first real parts of my career — appearing in a production of Clifford Odets's *Waiting for Lefty,* a prounion play being done at a Communist organization meeting hall in Montreal. Both Odets plays communicated a strong political philosophy, but I didn't care at all about that, and I suspect Leonard didn't either. At least not at that time. It was an opportunity to stand on a stage and act. That was all that mattered.

Many years later, Leonard's son, Adam, was making the transition from being an attorney to becoming a director. His TV career had gotten off to a good start when, he remembered, "I got an offer to do an independent production that I didn't think was going to lead anywhere. It felt like a step back, and I was going to turn it down when my dad asked me, 'Well, do you have

29

another offer to do something else?'

"I didn't, I told him.

" 'Well, then, take the job. You take the job because you need the job. You don't want any downtime. And number two, I guarantee you, you will either learn something from that job or you'll meet somebody on that job who's going to help you. You take the job. Don't turn down work if you don't have work to replace it.' "

If there is an actor's mantra that is it: take the job. We all lived by that, although for a long time most of us didn't live very well by it.

In 1949, Leonard was cast in the comedy *John Loves Mary* being done at a neighborhood temple. The director, Alysso Ristad, was a student at Boston College. Ristad invited the head of the school's theater program, a Jesuit priest, to see the play. Backstage, after the performance, the priest offered Leonard a half scholarship — valued at $37.50 — to attend a summer acting program at Boston College. That seemed like a great deal, but Leonard had to raise the other half, which actually was a substantial amount of money for him at the time. Leonard always described the West End as a village, a place where people looked out for each other. The head of another settlement house agreed to sponsor him. That program gave him the professional foundation he needed. He remembered, "It was a very enchanting eight weeks of theater, acting classes, helping build sets, learning how to design a set, how to light a set."

At the end of that summer, Leonard was offered a scholarship to attend the college, but he had already made up his mind: he was going to Hollywood to become an actor. It was a decision, he once said, that left his parents "grief stricken." An actor? Who becomes an actor? It's not a profession for a nice Jewish boy. Stay in Boston, they told him; go to college. Like most immigrant parents, they wanted him to have a real profession, preferably as a doctor or a lawyer. His older brother had gotten his college degree and become a chemical engineer, a real job, not like acting.

"My father's response was amazing," Leonard said. "He warned me, 'You'll be hanging around with gypsies and bums.' I understood that his vision of actors were the people who came into Iziaslav, in the villages and towns as a company, and did a performance in the town square and passed the hat — then maybe steal a loaf of bread, make love to the mayor's daughter, and leave in the morning. There was no future that he could see.

"And then he offered me one piece of advice, 'Learn to play the accordion.' Because if I could play the accordion, I could always make a living working bar mitzvahs and weddings. I was okay about that, because I understood what his thoughts were."

It was Leonard's grandfather who stood up to his parents, telling him to go and do and be, telling him to live his own life. Leonard always kept a little leather pouch with a zipper his grandfather had sewn from scraps, and it was one of his most valued possessions. "He was my guy," Leonard said about his grandfather.

Just imagine the desperate passion that Leonard must have felt to leave his parents and everyone he knew behind to go to California and take up this strange profession that in fact he knew so little about. The world was very different then. Hollywood existed as much as a fantasy as a real place. It wasn't easy to travel back and forth across the country; flying was much too expensive, and trains took several days. It was so expensive to call there that people in the east would wait until nighttime when the rates went down before telling the operator in solemn tones, "Long distance, please."

Maybe the hardest part of it was leaving

his mother. There was a Yiddish poem written by Itzik Manger that he loved. It's told by a young boy, who sees a tree "left alone, exposed to the storm." He decides that he will become a bird and rest on that tree and bring it comfort with his beautiful song. But his mother objects, crying, "Maybe you will freeze to death on the tree." So she makes him put on winter clothes and boots, a scarf, and a cap, and as a result, "I raise my wings to fly, it is too heavy for me . . . Her love hasn't let me become a bird." Leonard always identified with that poem. "I got away," he said, "but it was tough. It was very tough."

In addition to the $600 Leonard had saved from selling vacuum cleaners, he sold his prized possession, an electric-blue Ford, to his friend Henry Parker, and bought a $100 coach train ticket to Los Angeles. His parents went with him to the train station, and his mother stood there crying as the train pulled out. "I was an adventurer taking off for another world," he said. "To be an actor."

There really are only two places in America for actors to find work: Hollywood and New York. Hollywood was the center of the film industry; New York was the place for theater. The television industry was just beginning in both places, but for an actor, it wasn't considered either prestigious or important. A well-known actor's joke tells the story of several actors from New York who get in a car to head for California, while at the same time several Hollywood actors set out for New York. As these two cars pass each other in Kansas City, all the actors lean out the windows and shout, "Go back!"

Neither Leonard nor I became actors because we thought that someday we would be stars earning considerable fortunes. Leonard always said his goal had been to earn $10,000 a year as an actor; my goal was to earn $100 a week. It wasn't the possibility of stardom and money — there simply was nothing else we could do with our lives and feel fulfilled. It was who we were.

My experience was remarkably similar to Leonard's. I was in my third year at McGill University in Montreal when I told my father that I was going to be an actor. He was devastated. He tried to talk me out of it: "Acting isn't a respectable job for a man," he said. I wouldn't be able to earn a living at it. I'd be like one of those minstrels, never having a real home. Didn't I want a real life, with a home and a family? To his credit, he let me fly. When he finally accepted the fact that I was completely serious, he told me that, no matter what happened, there would always be a place for me. He asked only that I didn't become a hanger-on, someone who was dependent on other people or public assistance. That was his way of telling me to be a man.

While Leonard went west to California, I went south to New York. My career path was considerably different. I worked in summer stock in Canada and during the winter was a member of the Canadian National Repertory Theatre — a very, very minor member. But I was learning my craft every day. After three years, I was invited to join the Shakespeare Festival in Stratford, Ontario, which already was recognized as one of the finest rep companies in the world.

One day while I was driving to Toronto in a tremendous rainstorm and as I crossed a bridge, a mammoth eighteen wheeler coming from the other direction raced by me, spraying water from its front tire wells. The combination of a massive blast of water and the wind generated by the truck almost blew me into the Ottawa River. I realized something about myself at that moment: if my car went into the river, I would have left no tracks on this earth. Beyond my family, there was no one who truly cared about me. I had no close friends; I knew a lot of people, I'd worked and shared experiences with a lot of people, but there was no one who would miss me if I disappeared beneath the river. And conversely, there was no one other than my family that I cared enough about to miss if something happened to them. That understanding left me with a terribly empty feeling, but I didn't have the slightest idea what I could do to change that.

At Stratford, I eventually became a leading man. In 1955, my third season, we did Marlowe's *Tamburlaine the Great*. Anthony Quayle played the lead. I was the second lead. The play was so successful, we moved to the largest theater in New York, the Winter Garden. Our scheduled twelve-week run lasted only eight weeks, but by that point, I had been working regularly for several years and had proved that I could make a living as an actor. As long as I could survive on one meal a day.

It was much tougher for Leonard in Los Angeles. He enrolled at the once-respected Pasadena Playhouse but quickly was disillusioned. Students at the playhouse weren't eligible to perform on the main stage until their third year. Coincidently, they were doing a production of the same comedy Leonard had done in Boston, *John Loves Mary.* But as far as he was concerned, they weren't doing it as well. "I thought," he said, "I have to study here three years in order to do this level of work, and I'm already doing better work." After six months, he left, and within a couple of years, the school closed.

Go to law school and become a lawyer. Go to business school and become a businessman. Go to acting school and become a waiter, a cab driver, or — as in Leonard's case — work the counter in an ice cream parlor. Leonard moved into an inexpensive rooming house off the Sunset Strip. Most of the people living there were just like him, young actors looking for a break, or at least an agent. It was a grind; he went to all the talent agencies and casting agencies handing out his eight-by-ten head shot, looking for an opportunity. It was the same path that has been followed by countless young men and women hoping for the big break. Most times it never happens. It was a good thing his grandfather didn't get to check the soles of his shoes.

Leonard considered himself a character actor rather than a leading man. He always said his idols growing up were Paul Muni and Lon Chaney, actors who carefully crafted each one of their characters. Being a supporting actor rather than a lead was an interesting choice for Leonard. Once, thinking about that, he told an interviewer, "I'm a second child who was educated to the idea my older brother was to be given respect and not perturbed. I was not to upstage him. I was to give ground. So my acting career was designed to be a supporting player, a character actor." That seemed to be a part of Leonard's personality; while he certainly appreciated the benefits of his success, I never saw him act like a star. I actually remember thinking as I watched him at a *Star Trek* convention that on some level he seemed perplexed or even amused by the concept that fans adored him. Conversely, I was the only boy in our family; I had two sisters and a mother who adored me. I felt like a leading man in my childhood.

Leonard's problem was that agents were looking for leading-man types rather than supporting players. He couldn't find an agent to represent him, to send him out on casting calls, so he had to try to pick up work wherever he could find it. For example, one of his coworkers at the ice cream parlor introduced him to a producer on *The Pinky Lee Show,* a live half-hour children's show. It was the usual kid's comedy show, a little song, a little dance, a little seltzer down your pants. They also did short sketches. In Leonard Nimoy's first appearance on television as a professional actor, he played the role of Knuckles, a nasty crook pursuing Pinky Lee, whom he and his gang mistakenly believed had found the money they had stolen. He was called Knuckles because he continually cracked his knuckles — actually a sound effect created offstage by crunching strawberry boxes. They rehearsed for four days and performed the show the fourth night. For his performance he was paid fifteen dollars.

Now, obviously I didn't know Leonard then, but if there is one thing I am absolutely certain about, it is that he was the best possible Knuckles. I suspect no one ever cracked his knuckles more ominously. Leonard had total respect for his craft. He took every performance — even a broad comedy sketch on a children's show — seriously. Almost fifteen years later, when Gene Roddenberry hired him to create an alien with noticeably large ears, a character that in another actor's hands might well have become something quite different, it was exactly this same approach that imbued Spock with the dignity and humanity that made him so unique and appealing.

And when we first started working together, it was his personal investment in the character that almost caused a serious rift between us, when I made the mistake of treating Spock with less than complete respect. It was not a mistake I made a second time.

At that time, very few actors took television seriously. Leonard hadn't even seen TV until he moved into that rooming house. There was no real work on TV for a serious actor. It consisted primarily of people looking directly into the camera and talking or disc jockeys playing records. One camera would zoom in on the turntable and show the record spinning as the music played. When the song ended, the camera would focus on the disc jockey, who would say a few words, then put on another record.

Leonard made his second appearance on TV as a contestant on the show *Lights, Camera, Action.* Aspiring — and sometimes perspiring — young actors were handed a brief scene to do, and a panel judged their work. Showing how far television has come in sixty-five years, it was essentially the same format as shows like *American Idol* and *Dancing with the Stars.* In the sketch, Leonard was digging a hole in the basement of his home when his extremely irritating wife came downstairs and asked him what he

40

was doing. The answer, I suspect, was a malicious, knowing smile.

The winner that week was a singer who did a Broadway medley.

Television was something an actor did to pick up a few bucks while looking for real work on stage or, most importantly, in the movies. But nobody turned down work. As Leonard knew, every job came with the possibility that it might lead to something else. One day, for example, a young actress living in the rooming house asked Leonard, "Can you fence?" Not "Can you act?" but "Can you fence?" Fence? Of course. Who can't? I suspect she could have asked him anything short of "Can you fly an airliner?" and he would have responded seriously, "Of course." And he might have even said yes to the airliner, as he eventually became a skilled pilot. And, in fact, he had been in the fencing club in high school, although they used a thin foil as opposed to a broadsword.

He was cast as d'Artagnan in a children's theater production of *The Three Musketeers.* It ran for four Saturday mornings. There was no pay, but it was an opportunity to be on stage in front of an audience. An audience of children, but still an audience. Several weeks later, he went on an open

41

casting call for the movie version of a very popular radio and then television show entitled *Queen for a Day*. This was a show in which women competed to see who had the most difficult life. Each day several women would tell their sad story and describe their most desperate need. I've got nine kids and my washing machine broke. My car broke so I can't drive to work and my family is starving. Then the audience would vote on which one of them should be queen for a day and receive the necessary help. I suppose the other contestants just walked home. It was an awful concept, but the audience loved it. Maybe it made them feel better about the smaller difficulties of their own lives. When the casting director asked Leonard about his recent work, he replied that among other things he'd been in *The Three Muskeeters*.

The casting director's face lit up. "At the Coronet Theatre?"

Leonard nodded. "Yeah."

"I saw you," he said excitedly. "You were d'Artagnan, and you were wonderful." It turned out that show had been produced by a woman who had worked at the Goodman Theatre in Chicago with this casting director. *The Three Musketeers* turned out to be the first link in a chain that would stretch for decades.

In 1951, thanks to his swordplay, Leonard was cast in his first movie, *Queen for a Day.* He played the son of a contestant, a young man who had run away from home to join a carnival. It was a small part, and his name was incorrectly spelled "Nemoy," but it was a real film credit. It meant he was a working actor. That same year he played a supporting gangster in the movie *Rhubarb,* a comedy about a cat named Rhubarb who inherited a small fortune and a baseball team, the Brooklyn Loons.

Maybe because of his lanky, brooding look, Leonard began getting cast as a bad guy. He eventually played a crook or a gangster in a lot of B-movies. Many years later, he would claim that in his entire career he had never played a character anything at all like himself; Mr. Spock, for example, "didn't talk like me, look like me, walk like me, or act like me." But there was at least one role for which he was perfect. Coincidently, Boris Sagal also moved to LA, and the two men had become friends. He recommended Leonard for a part in a play being staged at the Wilshire Ebell Theatre. Leonard was perfect for it, Sagal said — they needed an actor who spoke a little Yiddish! The play ran for three performances, and

Leonard was paid thirty-five dollars. But it also made him one of the go-to actors in Hollywood when they needed someone who spoke Yiddish and worked cheap.

Unfortunately, there was little demand for an actor who spoke Yiddish and could duel. But in 1920, the founder of the great Yiddish Art Theatre in New York, Maurice Schwartz, came to LA to produce Sholem Aleichem's comedy *It's Hard to Be a Jew* in a theater on Los Sedalia Boulevard. Sholem Aleichem's Tevye became the basis of *Fiddler on the Roof*. This was sort of a homecoming for Schwartz, as he had directed a very successful version of the play at the Hollywood Civic Playhouse before World War II. If ever there was the perfect play for Leonard, this was it. Paul Muni had played the role on Second Avenue in New York. If there was one thing Leonard knew so well from his own experience, it was how hard it was to be a Jew. When Leonard went for his audition, Schwartz's wife looked at him and told her husband, in Yiddish, that he looked too much like a gentile to play a Jew.

Leonard responded in perfect Yiddish that he was very Jewish. Naturally, in a brilliant burst of typecasting, he was cast as the gentile. He had to dye his hair blond for the role. I've seen Leonard in numerous costumes and with all types of makeup; I've seen him as an alien, I've seen him as a 1930s Chicago gangster, but it is difficult for me to imagine him as a blond gentile. The plot line is that his character's Jewish friend sighs and tells him, "It's hard to be a Jew." Leonard's character doesn't think it is so difficult, so they make a bet that he can pose as a Jew. Naturally, hilarity ensues. It's the traditional gefilte-fish-out-of-water story. The play ran for a few months, and during that time, Leonard became close to Schwartz. "He was a wonderful theater man," Leonard remembered. "He was brave on stage; he was big, he was bold, he was theatrical. Given an opportunity on stage he would get hold of it . . . and chew it!"

Perhaps more importantly, he wrote a long letter to Leonard's parents in Boston, telling them to stop worrying so much. A letter from Schwartz was a big deal. Maurice Schwartz was a big *macher.* He wanted to be Leonard's theatrical father, he wrote, and assured them that their son was a nice kid and he was going to be fine.

What Leonard did not dare tell his parents was that he had stopped going to shul. That was a big deal for him and probably would have been difficult for them. A few months after arriving in Los Angeles, he had bought a ticket for the High Holy Day services being held in the Shrine Auditorium. He walked in expecting to find a welcoming communal atmosphere; instead, the first thing they did was raise funds for some cause. He was shocked — and stood up and walked out. His experience had been that a shul was a place for a community of people to come together to celebrate meaningful rituals. This was more like the department-store version of religious observance. Many years later, my wife and I would go with Leonard and his second wife, Susan, to his synagogue to celebrate those holidays. My religious experience was different from his; my father spoke Yiddish, but I didn't. And while my sisters continued to keep kosher when they had their own homes, I didn't. I was more a spiritual person than a religious person. But there was something wonder-fully familial about sitting in synagogue next to Leonard and praying with him. His great love of the traditions and his respect for the history that brought us there together on those holidays was quite meaningful. When I was with him on those days, I could understand why he was so appalled about what he perceived to be the commercializa-tion of religion.

While working on *It's Hard to Be a Jew,*

Leonard met a lovely young woman actress named Sandi Zober, who was working as an understudy. She had the kind of exotic background that must have appealed to him; her parents had emigrated from Latvia and somehow ended up in Cordova, Alaska, where she was born and raised. It was a small town that could be reached only by plane or boat. She had that kind of creative exuberance that hadn't been dulled by growing up in a large city. She had moved to Los Angeles when she was sixteen and graduated from USC. Leonard always had an inquisitive mind. He was open to possibilities; he always wanted to know more. And Sandi, as I got to know her, was very much the same type of person. They married while he was on leave from the army in 1954. Being married in those days was something people did; I did it myself in 1956. I was starring in a CBC play I'd written, and a beautiful young woman named Gloria Rosenberg was cast opposite me as the beautiful female lead. She was known professionally as Gloria Rand, as Rosenberg carried with it a certain . . . a certain Rosenberg. This acting business brings together a lot of good-looking young people, and many of them pair off. We were married four months after we'd met. In the 1950s, people married for better and for worse and for life. Or so we believed. The general belief in the acting community was that two people could starve as easily as one. So when Leonard and I met, we both had been married more than a decade.

Although in the early 1950s I was working more regularly than Leonard, I'm quite sure we shared that trait most common among young actors, an unshakable belief that no matter how impossible it seemed at times, whatever it took, we were going to be successful. Success was easy to measure: paying the monthly rent on time. The confidence and resiliency of young actors is amazing: they go to bed every night believing tomorrow is going to be the day. So we lived from job to job, eating the least expensive items on the menu, learning the craft. But if someone had asked Leonard or me, "How can you do this?" I have no doubt at all that both of us would have responded, "How can you *not* do this?"

Every single job mattered. Leonard earned a reputation as a good actor who showed up on time every day, knew his lines, and caused no problems, very desirable traits. Most often, he played the heavy — off beat, nasty guys glowering in the background who said very little. They said very little because the pay scale changed after five lines. He also played ethnic characters — Latinos and Native Americans, for example.

Eventually, he was even able to sign with a Hollywood agent. This was not one of the large agencies; it was a hardworking guy who lived in a trailer in one of the canyons. He sent Leonard to audition for a low-budget movie called *Kid Monk Beroni.* Leonard sat in the waiting room all afternoon; one thing every actor eventually becomes an expert in is waiting. His name was never called because he wasn't on the list. I suspect in every actor's career he has heard those words: "You're not on the list." My first major movie role was as Alexi Karamazov in director Richard Brooks's *The Brothers Karamazov.* It was an incredible opportunity. The cast included great actors like Yul Brynner, Lee J. Cobb, and Claire Bloom. *I've made it,* I thought as I drove up to the front gate at MGM. It would be impossible to express how proud and excited I felt at that moment. It would not have surprised me to hear trumpets heralding the appearance of this young soon-to-be star. The guard, a man whose name I shall never forget, Ken Hollywood, looked at his clipboard, shook his head, and said those memorable words: "You're not on the list."

I turned around and went home.

Leonard didn't leave, however. He talked his way into the room and got the title role. This was his first major role. He played a disfigured Italian kid from the Bronx whose appearance leaves him with a chip on his shoulder. Under the direction of the kindly parish priest, he becomes a successful boxer and meets two women, one of whom steals his money. Eventually, he saves enough for plastic surgery and ends up with the sweet and supportive girl from his neighborhood who has always loved him.

The film had a ten-day shooting schedule but was finished in nine. Leonard was paid $350 plus the suits he wore. He also got his first review in *Variety;* the most memorable thing about this film, the reviewer wrote, was that "it serves to introduce a young actor named Leonard Nimoy in the title role. He is a capable juve who merits attention."

There is no best way to build a career. As an actor, Leonard once told an interviewer, "You're always out of work and looking for the next job. Even while you were working you were worrying about what you were going to do next." Oddly, Leonard wasn't an especially good athlete, but after playing a professional boxer, he played a football player in *Francis Goes to West Point* —

Francis being a famed talking mule. Then, he played an alien for the first time in his life in the Republic Pictures serial *Zombies of the Stratosphere,* which consisted of twelve fifteen-minute cliffhanging episodes to draw kids to the movies each Saturday. Leonard played Narab, one of three villainous zombies from Mars who come to Earth intending to blast it out of its orbit so Mars can fill that space. They arrived on Earth in a cigar-shaped spaceship that wobbled across the silver screen, leaving a trail of white smoke, dressed in what looked like latex sweatsuits with hoods covering most of their faces. Leonard's costume had a sprayed-on rubber surface that made it so rigid it took several men to pull it on. And the rubber didn't breathe, so it was really hot; it was so hot that every few hours, they would have to take a break to pour the puddles of perspiration out of their boots. That role actually turned out to be excellent preparation for *Star Trek.*

Naturally, as a leading-man type who was emoting in great Shakespearean dramas as a member of a celebrated Canadian National Repertory Theatre, I wouldn't have appeared in anything like *Zombies of the Stratosphere.* Instead, the series I was in at just about the same time Leonard was doing that was called *Space Command*. Like Leonard, it was my first time in outer space. *Space Command* was a TV series made by the Canadian Broadcasting Corporation. According to the announcer's opening, "[These are tales of] the infinitesimal lives of men dedicated to the planet Earth and its perilous . . . Space Command!" While Leonard was coming from Mars, we were going to Mars. The most memorable aspect of that show was that one of the leads was James Doohan. It was the first time we worked together. Maybe it wasn't Shakespeare, but for me, it was far more important — it was a job.

While most Americans had this image of Hollywood being a glamorous place where actors often worked with stars like Ava Gardner, Lana Turner, Clark Gable, and John Wayne, that was not Leonard's world or my world. The real world was about going to as many auditions as possible and taking what was offered without being discouraged. Just imagine the challenge of trying to play a Martian zombie in a latex suit with integrity! It was the humorist Will Rogers who gave what might be the best advice to a young actor I've ever heard. In the early 1930s, in the middle of the Depression, Rogers ran into John Wayne on the same Republic Pictures lot. Wayne looked very unhappy, and Rogers asked him what was wrong. "Oh, they've got me playing a singing cowboy in these western serials," Wayne began and then complained about the dumb roles he was getting. Rogers listened patiently until Wayne finished, then asked, "You working?"

Wayne nodded his head. "Yeah," he said.

"Keep working," Rogers told him, then kept walking.

Leonard kept working. In Republic's western with music *The Old Overland Trail,* he played Chief Black Hawk and got a nice billing just below star Rex Allen's horse, Koko. In the classic horror film *Them!,* he was a soldier passing along a strange report that a pilot had spotted giant ants the size of flying saucers, a report Sergeant Nimoy laughed off — unfortunately for civilization, as the ominous musical soundtrack suggested.

That role actually prepared him for his command performance as a member of the United States Army. Rather than being drafted, in 1953, he enlisted in the Army Reserve, which meant he had to serve two years of active duty. After completing basic training at Fort Ord, California, he was shipped to Fort Benning, Georgia, for ranger training. It was there, in hand-to-hand combat training, that he first encountered the paralyzing Vulcan neck pinch.

Okay, that's not true, but the concept of Leonard with a rifle and a bayonet is difficult for me to imagine. He was as tough as he needed to be, and you always had the feeling if pushed too far, he was very capable of defending himself. But that wasn't his essence. So after two months at Benning, he wrote to several commanders suggesting that there might be a better use for someone with his experience. Incredibly, there was. The army knew fighting; it did not know television. Television was tough. They intended to produce a weekly, hour-long show featuring talented soldiers. Leonard was asked to write and produce it; and within a few weeks, he was transferred to Fort McPherson, just outside Atlanta, and reclassified as a military entertainment specialist. The show never got on the air, but Leonard spent the rest of his time in the service writing, directing, hosting, and even narrating an array of army programming.

Leonard being Leonard, though, serving in the army, getting married, and having his first child, his daughter, Julie, wasn't enough for him. He was constantly moving forward, always working or taking classes or, later, teaching classes. When he got off duty at five o'clock, he began acting and directing for a small amateur theater group that later gained recognition as the Atlanta Theatre Guild. Among the plays he directed and starred in there was *A Streetcar Named Desire.* The hardest thing for Leonard to do was nothing. His son, Adam, described his father as someone whose life "was about working and activity and finding those things he was passionate about and doing them. It was in his blood. It wasn't a conscious choice; artists have to stay busy and continually challenge themselves to create. He wasn't simply an actor; he also was a writer, a very successful film director, and I think he was only really happy when he was working.

"Even when he was in downtime at home he never just sat around; he always was building something, paving something, re-landscaping something, making furniture. He always was on the go."

Two very important things happened while Leonard was in the service. First, as he explained, the army made a big man out of him: "When I enlisted I was at the stage physically where I was beyond playing juveniles and not yet mature enough to play adult roles." His physical growth and the maturity he gained allowed him to play a much broader range of characters. And the second thing that happened was television, television, and more television.

In the early 1950s, television was a luxury that not many people could afford. Often one person in a building had a set, and he or she would invite the neighbors in to watch the popular shows, usually leaving the door open so people could stand in the hallway and watch. Bars that installed TVs did great business. Because the possible viewership was limited, so was programming. In 1951, there were only 108 stations in 62 cities covering 35 states. By the time Leonard was discharged, the audience had more than doubled and television had expanded throughout the nation. Networks were running "spectacular" events; in 1955 NBC's *Peter Pan,* starring Mary Martin, attracted an incredible sixty million viewers. By 1955, more than half of all Americans had TV sets. In 1956, sixteen thousand TV sets were being bought every day. That created the need for more programming, which, in turn, created the need for more actors.

The three major networks dominated the industry, but there were independent stations scattered throughout the country —

and there was a real shortage of programming. Initially, television was radio with pictures; often, shows consisted of little more than someone looking into the camera and talking. The large movie studios were reluctant to sell their old movies to television, believing that would keep people out of the theaters. Neither the networks nor the independent stations could afford to produce enough programming to fill twenty-four hours, so they simply put a camera on a test pattern and signed off for the night. To fill that void, numerous production companies began creating original shows that they could sell to stations in each market. Frederick Ziv had been creating and syndicating radio programming since 1937. In 1948, Ziv Television became the first TV syndication company. Ziv's first show, an anthology series named *Fireside Theater,* aired for the first time in 1949. Leonard's last job before entering the army was an appearance in a *Fireside Theater* episode entitled "A Man of Peace." It was the story of a famous fencing master who retired after an accident, refusing to duel again, until he had to prove he was not a coward by fighting his star pupil. I can guess how Leonard got that part.

By 1955, Ziv had become one of the

industry's most successful syndication companies. It was producing more than 250 low-budget half-hour TV episodes a year, which made it one of the most important producers in television. An entire show usually was shot in two or three days. Directors and actors moved easily and often between Ziv shows. Leonard was discharged from the army into what became known as the Golden Age of Television.

# THREE

Steve Guttenberg was directed by Leonard in the hit comedy *Three Men and a Baby.* It's the story of three bachelors — played by Guttenberg, Tom Selleck, and Ted Danson — who have to take care of a baby left by one of their girlfriends. It's generally accepted among actors that the hardest thing to do is work with animals and babies. When I asked Guttenberg if that was true, he smiled and shook his head. "That's not true at all," he said. "The hardest thing is not working."

After being discharged, Leonard and Sandi, who was pregnant with their second child, their son, Adam, rented a small apartment on La Cienega, and Leonard went right to work — driving a cab. He knew it might take time to get reestablished, and they needed to pay the rent. Driving a cab, like waiting tables, was the perfect job for an actor. He could work at night while going to auditions during the day, and when he got a part, he could quit without being missed. "I did that kind of work for a long time," he said. "I didn't want to take a responsible job where people depended on me. If I did take a job where there was any dependency on me, I would let them know I could leave abruptly. I'm an actor!"

I actually never knew Leonard drove a cab until much later in our lives, when he just happened to mention that he had driven a cab in the same neighborhood in which he then lived. And then he told me about his most memorable passenger and what he had learned from him. Democratic senator Adlai Stevenson, then trying to get the party's presidential nomination after losing to Eisenhower in 1952, was speaking at a political dinner being held at the Beverly Hilton. Leonard was told to pick up a passenger at the Bel Air Hotel. That passenger turned out to be Massachusetts senator John F. Kennedy. When Kennedy found out Leonard was from Boston, he barraged Leonard with questions about the West End, about his parents' immigrant experience, and about Leonard's acting career. Leonard told him it was tough, then asked him about Stevenson's chances of getting the nomination for a second time. Rather than answering, Kennedy leaned forward and said, "You talk to a lot of people. What do you think?"

When they reached the Hilton, something else memorable happened: Kennedy tried to stiff him for the $1.25 fare. "He stepped out of the cab and started to walk away without paying. By this time, he'd been distracted." One thing about Leonard, when he did the work, he expected to be paid. And as I would learn, he was willing to fight for what he believed he was owed. So Leonard got out of his cab and followed Kennedy into the hotel. "I want my $1.25," he said. Kennedy found someone he knew and borrowed $3, which he handed to Leonard.

That trip actually had an impact on his life. The fact that rather than answering Leonard's question, Kennedy turned it around and "made me feel much more worthwhile — more meaningful and important to myself; that a man in his position would ask me for my opinion. He obviously knew much more than I did, but he wasn't interested in impressing me with his knowledge . . . That was one of the most important lessons I ever learned, and often I found myself doing exactly what he did. If somebody asks me a question, I may have an answer, but often I'll say, 'But what do you think?' I learn a lot more that way than simply by answering the question myself."

That really became an important part of his personality. Anyone who spent time with Leonard would pick up on that immediately. John de Lancie accurately described him as "a formidable listener. He listened actively, which most people don't do."

His first year out of the army, he was cast in several Ziv shows; he was a cowboy in *Luke and the Tenderfoot,* a sailor in *Navy Log,* he did an episode of *Your Favorite Story* and an episode of *The Man Called X,* a spy story supposedly based on the true adventures of a government adventurer. He also appeared on stage, playing a supporting role in a play entitled *Life Is but a Dream* at the Civic Playhouse, a show that would have been long forgotten except that Leonard got his first strong review in the *LA Times:* "Leonard Nimoy carries conviction."

No one who knew Leonard would disagree with that either; in everything he did, he always carried conviction.

I actually made my debut on American television at that time. I was offered a key role on one of the most popular shows in television's brief history: I created the role of Ranger Bob on *The Howdy Doody Show,* costarring with several marionettes and a clown named Clarabell. Clarabell did not speak; instead he expressed his opinions by honking a bicycle horn. That did cut down on meaningful dialogue.

Before coming to New York, I had done several shows on the CBC. In my first major role, I had costarred with the great Basil Rathbone in a live version of Melville's tragedy *Billy Budd.* Rathbone had created the role of Sherlock Holmes in the movies, and I probably had seen every picture he'd made. It was a tremendous opportunity for me to learn from a respected veteran actor. Admittedly, I was probably a little nervous, as an estimated ten million Canadians would be watching. The performance seemed to be going very well until that moment Rathbone stepped onto the ship and somehow managed to get his foot caught in a large bucket. While the camera shot him only from the waist up, he was madly shaking his leg trying to get the bucket off. Naturally, he forgot his lines, and when an actor forgets his lines, he begins to sweat. So the great Basil Rathbone, whom I had admired for so long, was standing there shaking a bucket off his foot while sweat poured down his face as he tried to remember his lines. Never in the history of performance has anyone literally tried to act normally with so little success.

But that was quite typical of the things that happened in the early days of television. While Leonard was in Hollywood doing mostly Ziv shows, I was in New York doing live television. While he was playing Native Americans, I was working regularly on Sunday morning religious shows like *Lamp Unto My Feet*. While I continued learning my craft by rehearsing and working, Leonard believed in learning how to act by studying acting.

I didn't take acting classes. Not that I didn't recognize their value, but I learned by doing; Leonard studied his craft. Leonard spent most of his career refining his craft. I actually think Leonard's acting ability often was underrated, primarily because he made it look so easy. Spock, for example, seemed to be easy to imitate — but it took great skill to create that blatant dispassion. Just before joining the army, for example, he had joined a group of young actors forming a company so they might work onstage. One member of that group, it turned out, was James Arness, and he and Leonard became very friendly. A year later, Arness happened to be in Atlanta promoting a movie he'd made with John Wayne, and Leonard called him. Arness told Leonard he'd just signed to star in a new cowboy series based on the popular radio show *Gun-smoke*.

Two years later, James Arness was a major television star. That wasn't too surprising. We were surrounded by that kind of success, so we knew it was possible. So we kept working and hoping that eventually our turn would come. Later, people would remark how amazing it was that Leonard and I appeared together in an episode of *U.N.C.L.E.* It wasn't at all amazing; we worked so often with so many different people that it might have been more unusual if we had never done the same show.

Leonard had resumed taking acting classes when he got back to LA, this time with an actor named Jeff Corey. Corey was a very talented actor who had been blacklisted, meaning he was suspected of having Communist sympathies, so no producer would hire him. So he opened an acting school and was well respected. Among the students who Leonard became friends with was Vic Morrow, who eventually starred in the series *Combat!* That was another link in that long chain that eventually would make all the difference in the galaxies to Leonard's career.

As incredible as it may seem, most of us were only vaguely aware of the blacklist. I don't remember ever talking with him about it. It was one of those subjects that just didn't seem to affect our lives, even though we were right in the middle of it. As Leonard once explained, we were young, naïve, and so totally preoccupied with trying to earn a living that we paid little attention to it. Leonard, who eventually became very politically active in progressive causes, told an interviewer much later in his life, "I'm shocked that there was so much of that going on around Hollywood and I was so totally out of touch with it." He remembers having to get an FBI clearance to play a bit part on the show *West Point.* I'm not sure I ever did, maybe because I wasn't an American citizen.

When the blacklist was finally lifted, Corey began working again, eventually costarring in many movies like *Butch Cassidy and the Sundance Kid, True Grit,* and *Little Big Man.* Leonard had been studying with Corey for more than two years when Corey finally was able to resume his career; when Corey went back to work, Leonard began teaching some of his classes. After doing that for a couple of years, Leonard opened his own acting studio. Among his students were pop singers Fabian and Bobby Vee, as well as Alex Rocco, who played the role of casino owner

Moe Greene in *The Godfather.* Originally, the Italian Rocco auditioned for the part of a gangster, but Leonard apparently was such a fine teacher that director Francis Ford Coppola auditioned the Italian Rocco and decided, "I got my Jew!"

Leonard was a highly trained actor; I was not. Our acting techniques were quite different. In his studio, Leonard taught his version of the then very popular technique known as Method acting. Until that time, acting styles were very broad, often verging on melodramatic. It was very formulaic acting, sort of like acting off a menu of choices. Method acting, which Lee Strasberg had made famous at the Actors Studio in New York and Leonard was teaching in his studio, taught students to "become" the character and express that character's real emotions. It meant studying the character's social, physical, and psychological condition. It meant learning as much as possible about the character, even if the actor had to create that backstory himself to understand the character's — here it comes — motivation. It meant deciding what clothes the character would wear that accurately reflected his or her personality. It meant utilizing body language years before anybody even used that term. It was revolutionary;

rather than showing the character's emotion, the actor actually had to feel it.

An actor's knowledge of his character started with the script. Leonard always was in awe of the written word, and when he himself wrote, he brought the same diligence and respect to the page as he did to his performance. The script should provide clues to the actor about who his or her character is, what process this person is going through, and how he or she responds. An actor also had to understand the purpose of each scene, "the spine of the scene" he called it, what knowledge is supposed to be conveyed to audience through the action and dialogue in each scene. And then the subtext — what is the intention of each line? What is the character really trying to say? Once an actor understands that, he or she can layer the performance in terms of bringing both voice and mannerisms to that moment. "There are numerous ways of saying, 'I love you,' " he would explain. How it might be said depends on the situation and the actor's overall objective. If, for example, a man is telling a woman for the very first time that he loves her, it requires complete devotion; if, on the other hand, it's a way of ending an argument, it would be said a very different way.

An actor trained in that technique, Leonard believed, would always bring honesty to the role. "A character is like a plant," he said. "The richer the soil, the better it grows. One of an actor's jobs is to nourish his plants." In 1977, for example, he was hired to follow Richard Burton, Anthony Hopkins, and Tony Perkins as child psychiatrist Martin Dysart in the Broadway hit *Equus*. It's a difficult role in the complex story of the psychiatrist hired to treat a young boy who blinded six horses for some unknown reason. To properly prepare for the role, Leonard advertised in *The New York Times*, looking for a "horse psychiatrist to help in research." He received more than two hundred responses from psychologists, veterinarians, trainers, jockeys, and gamblers. He hired an ethologist, a person who studies animal behavior, and, he said, he "came away with a feeling of awe at the power of the horse in the night mind of man."

To me, describing acting as a technique has always seemed kind of . . . technical. Meanwhile, my technique is quite different; it is the classic nontechnical technique: I memorized the script and played the character. I tried to find the core of my character, the one word, the one line in the script that best described that character's intentions, and then moved out from that. Like Leonard, I found clues in the script. My hope is that I can characterize something with enough emphasis that it is very different from myself, the actor. If I could make that core line real, then the rest of the character would follow. Too often, the actor bleeds through his or her portrayal and the character becomes just another version of other characters he or she has played with just a different name and a different costume. When Leonard and I began working together, we approached the material from very different places, but fortunately, perhaps because of the nature of the characters, it worked beautifully. But by then, both of us had been working regularly for a long time.

As an acting teacher and coach, as well as a working actor, Leonard became part of LA's community of young actors. Like every other business in the world, relationships are important in the entertainment industry. Soon after Leonard was discharged, Boris Sagal, for example, cast him in an episode of *Matinee Theater* that he was directing. *Matinee Theater* was a daily live hour-long dramatic show. There were four days of rehearsals and then the actual performance, so there were always five shows in progress at the same time. That meant a lot of work for actors. Sagal hired Leonard for an under-five-line part in a drama starring Vincent Price. Price played his normal madman role, a husband planning to blow up his wife by filling the house with gas, then rigging the phone to spark when he called. Leonard played a nosy deliveryman.

He was hired for another episode, but the director wasn't comfortable with Leonard's choices, and he was replaced. That was devastating for Leonard. He didn't do anything casually. Even when he had only a single line, he worked at it, so to be told he wasn't good enough or he didn't understand the character was a real attack on his integrity. He was fighting to establish a career, and this was a big step backward. It actually took him some time to get over it.

Because of the way he worked, in some ways these bit parts were more difficult for him than larger roles. The more dialogue a character has, the easier it is to become comfortable in the role. With only three or four lines, it's hard to establish any rhythm or create a believable character. But it was work, it came with a paycheck, and so he never turned down an offer and tried his best to create something. In *Get Smart,* for example, he played a sinister character lurking in the back of a poolroom. So he wore dark clothes and dark sunglasses — this was long before people wore sunglasses inside — and kept the sunglasses on throughout the entire episode. Ironically, the one thing he was rarely permitted to do on camera was smoke. Leonard was a heavy smoker off camera; in fact, a lot of actors were, as it helped them relax between takes. I smoked too. Once, he was playing an outlaw in a western and asked the propman for one of the hand-rolled brown cigarettes cowboys smoked. He intended to use it to help create his character. The propman turned him down. Ziv was churning out these shows without knowing which companies might end up sponsoring them. They were concerned that cigarette companies might not be willing to sponsor a program if bad guys were seen using their product, so bad guys didn't smoke in those shows. Only heroes relaxed with a cigarette.

As a character actor, Leonard played an amazing array of characters, although his specialty was being the heavy, the bad guy. While some Ziv shows would not use actors more than once, other shows were far more relaxed about it. He did eight episodes of Lloyd Bridges's *Sea Hunt,* for example, playing everything from a revolutionary student to an explosives thief. In one episode, he would have a mustache; in another, he'd take off the mustache and wear a hat. He did a variety of accents, whatever it took to earn a paycheck. Most Ziv shows paid $80 a day and were shot in two days; *Sea Hunt* was one of their most successful shows, so it had a larger budget — they paid $100 a day and shot in two and a half days, so if they needed a Spaniard with a mustache and glasses, Leonard said, *"Sí, señor,"* pasted on the mustache, and wore glasses. During the next few years, Leonard appeared in many of the most successful series on television, working with some of our best actors — and gaining a reputation in the business as a go-to bad guy.

He became a regular on westerns, playing both cowboys and Native Americans, appearing in *Colt .45, Tombstone Territory, The Rough Riders, Mackenzie's Raiders, 26 Men, Tate* — the adventures of a one-armed gunfighter — *Outlaws, Death Valley Days, Cimarron City,* three episodes of *Broken Arrow, Tales of Wells Fargo, The Rebel,* and Doug McClure's *The Virginian.* He worked with Academy Award winner Ernest Borgnine in one of his four appearances on

*Wagon Train,* Clint Eastwood's *Rawhide, Bonanza,* and of course four episodes of Jim Arness's *Gunsmoke,* as well as all the others. He played a soldier in Dean Stockwell's infantry platoon on the last day of World War II on *The Twilight Zone,* a submariner on three episodes of *The Silent Service,* and a sailor on *Navy Log.* He played both cops and robbers, he did two episodes of the science-fiction show *The Outer Limits,* and he worked on medical shows from *General Hospital* to *Dr. Kildare.*

A lot of professionalism and little money went into these shows. There was no time for preparation or rehearsal; you just did it. When these shows went on location, they shot from sunup to the last light. They literally would chase the sunlight, running away from the encroaching shadows. The crew would take the camera and reflectors and run up a hill, staying just ahead of the shadow, stopping and shooting for a minute, then picking up and moving another ten feet. Close-ups were often shot against a wall so they could be done after the sun went down simply by lighting a small area. If there was a way to save money, they figured it out. They didn't deceive themselves into believing they were creating art; they were making television shows.

"It was great training," Leonard once said. If you flubbed a line or made a mistake, the camera kept rolling, then they would go back and just pick it up one line earlier. There were no lengthy retakes, no second or third takes of a scene. Often the actors didn't know the context of the scene when it was shot. It was make your entrance, do your exit. Then they shot the close-ups. That was the one chance to show any kind of expression. He believed that "whether or not you got called back had to do with whether or not you could hit your marks and say your lines on demand. I tried very hard to be proficient at that so I would be invited back.

"I remember doing an episode of *M Squad,* a cop show starring Lee Marvin. I played an arsonist; my brother was played by James Coburn. We worked together for three or four days. One morning we were supposed to be in makeup at 7:30 and on the set, ready to go, at eight o'clock. I got there on time, no Jim Coburn. Eight o'clock, I'm made up, ready to go, on the set, no Jim Coburn. I heard through the buzz that he had overslept. That was unheard of that an actor would hold up a television company. We scrambled and did some other things. I thought, oh this poor guy just ruined his career. We finished the episode and Jim Coburn's next job was in the movie *The Magnificent Seven.* He became this big hot star and I remember saying to myself, I was on time; where's my stardom!"

Leonard was not a star, he never got top billing, but he worked regularly. He took whatever was offered. On the first of his three appearances on *Broken Arrow,* for example, he played a Native American accused of a hanging crime — and he had no lines. He spent most of the show sitting in the prisoner's dock listening silently to testimony.

Like the majority of actors, Leonard continued to work at other jobs to support his career. In addition to teaching acting and driving a cab, at various times he ran a vending machine route, delivered newspapers, was a movie usher, and even worked in a pet shop selling exotic fish. It was never an easy life, and as he pointed out, "I went a long time before I could make a living as an actor. Before *Star Trek,* I spent about fifteen years in Los Angeles looking for work as an actor, and during that time, I never had a job that lasted any longer than two weeks."

Those were the "character-building years," as Leonard later referred to them, and every person who has ever tried to earn a living in this profession can relate to that — and knows how hard it is to maintain the dream. Even he admitted that at times he would be very unhappy, very angry. Those feelings are part of an actor's life; you see people you've worked with, people whose talent you doubt or you know aren't as good as you, get parts that you should be playing or on occasion even become stars. At times, you begin to wonder, *Why not me?* It often is more frustration than jealousy, but you just keep going. It affects every part of your life. Sometimes, though, that frustration explodes. Leonard's wife Sandi once told an interviewer, "We had terrible fights. There were times he wanted to give up acting and take a sensible job, and I wouldn't let him." Believe me, every struggling actor's family can relate to Sandi when she continued, "Leonard wasn't much fun in those days. And I didn't always appreciate what a strong husband and father he was."

Few of those small roles gave Leonard a chance to really apply his talents, so he found other ways to exercise his skills. In 1962, he and his good friend Vic Morrow optioned the movie rights to a play they had done in a small theater on Santa Monica Boulevard, Jean Genet's *Deathwatch*. It wasn't exactly a hot commercial property. Rather it was a complex, highly emotional story that takes place in a jail cell in which two prisoners are fighting over the affections of the third inmate, who happens to be a killer. He had gotten wonderful reviews in that play and often credited it with getting him noticed in the industry, and after that, he began working a lot more often. It marked the first time he was able to earn enough as an actor to cut back on his other jobs. Following that, his performance onstage in Genet's better-known play *The Balcony* consolidated his growing reputation as a talented young actor.

Leonard and Morrow somehow raised $125,000 from small contributors to shoot the film. Just think about that: Leonard was working several jobs and barely earning a living, yet his respect for his profession and his passion for honest and emotional storytelling was so profound that he spent his energies — and probably most of his money — getting this project completed. I can't imagine that anyone believed this film was going to be a commercial blockbuster. They began filming *Deathwatch* in 1964 with Morrow directing and Paul Mazursky and Michael Forest costarring with Leonard, while Gavin MacLeod played a minor role.

They couldn't find a distributor, so they booked into select theaters themselves. It opened in San Francisco in 1966. Two years later, after Leonard began to get some recognition, they managed to get limited distribution in art houses nationally.

As it turned out, one of the people who saw that play in Santa Monica was a young actor named George Takei. He was so taken with the performance that he remembered the names of the actors, and when Roddenberry cast him in the role of Lieutenant Hikaru Sulu, he immediately recognized the name Leonard Nimoy.

I had also started working regularly on television, making guest-starring appearances in many of them. Live drama was very popular and even a little prestigious at that time, and initially, I appeared regularly in shows presented by a single sponsor like *The Kaiser Aluminum Hour, Alcoa Premiere, Goodyear Playhouse, Kraft Theatre, The United States Steel Hour,* and *The DuPont Show of the Month,* as well as legendary programs like *Playhouse 90, Alfred Hitchcock Presents,* and two classic episodes of *The Twilight Zone.* While I continued making movies, television was where the work was, and as a new father, I needed to keep working. Eventually, I worked at least once on practically every memorable show from that period, among them *Naked City, 77 Sunset Strip,* and *Route 66.* On *The Outer Limits,* I was an astronaut returned from orbiting Venus who can't seem to get warm. I appeared regularly on *The Defenders* and actually was offered the leading role. On *The Fugitive,* I played a former police officer running a youth program, who also may be a serial killer responsible for several murders that Richard Kimball is accused of committing. I appeared on medical shows like *Dr. Kildare.* On *Gunsmoke,* I played a wanted man pursued by Marshal Dillon hiding out among the Quakers. None of us had the slightest idea we were in the middle of television's Golden Age.

When you worked as often Leonard and I did, eventually you would cross paths with many different people. You never knew when one of them might be in a position to make a difference in your career. In 1960, for example, Leonard guest-starred as a deputy sheriff on western writer Sam Peeples's show, *The Tall Man.* It starred Barry Sullivan and Clu Gulager as Pat Garrett and Billy the Kid. That episode was the first one written by a twenty-one-year-old woman named Dorothy C. Fontana, and she was so excited, she went to the set to meet the actor. She recalled, "I told Leonard this was the first thing I had ever sold, and he asked me some questions and was very encouraging and polite. The producers liked his character and the way he did it, so they brought him back for a second episode. But then they killed him, and he was off the show."

The magic struck Leonard's friend from Jeff Corey's classes, Vic Morrow, who starred in the successful World War II action series *Combat!* Morrow helped Leonard get a nice role in an episode entitled "The Wounded Don't Cry." He was cast as Private Neumann, a GI who translates German — thank you, Yiddish — when his battalion finds an enemy aid station. Among the viewers when the show was broadcast was a casting director named Joe D'Agosta, who really appreciated Leonard's performance. D'Agosta kept good notes about who was being hired to do what, his way of finding talented young actors. Not too long afterward, D'Agosta was doing the casting for producer Gene Roddenberry's first show, *The Lieutenant*. *The Lieutenant* was the story of a Marine infantry battalion stationed at Camp Pendleton during peacetime. The title character was platoon leader and training instructor Second Lieutenant

William Tiberius Rice.

Tiberius? What an interesting middle name for a character. But where have I heard that name before? Oh, I remember — a great Roman emperor.

In the episode entitled "In the Highest Tradition," Leonard played a slick Hollywood producer who wants to use the facilities at Pendleton to shoot a film about a Marine hero — who turns out to be somewhat less than heroic. Also appearing in that hour-long show were Gary Lockwood as the lieutenant and Majel Barrett. It was directed by Marc Daniels, whom Leonard had met previously when Daniels was directing an episode of *Dr. Kildare* featuring Leonard's acting student Fabian. This kind of flamboyant producer was not normally the type of part Leonard played, but his agent, Alex Brewis, was known for his persistence. D'Agosta once described him as "a likable bulldog." No matter what D'Agosta was casting, Brewis would show up in his office telling him, "That's the perfect role for Leonard. You got to bring him in for it." It didn't matter what it was. "That's perfect for Leonard." D'Agosta remembered being impressed with Leonard's work in *Combat!* and brought him in to read for the part. While initially Marc Daniels didn't think he was right for the role, Leonard's audition convinced Daniels to give Leonard the part. Leonard said that this turned out to be the most important audition of his life. It was a small decision that had enormous ramifications.

*The Lieutenant* turned out to be the stepping-stone to *Star Trek* for several people. *Star Trek* was the next program Gene Roddenberry produced, and he asked D'Agosta to help him with the casting. Majel Barrett married Roddenberry and appeared in every version of *Star Trek,* both on television and in the movies, often both as a character and the voice of the computer. Gary Lockwood costarred in the second *Star Trek* pilot and several years later appeared with me in my series *T.J. Hooker.* Marc Daniels eventually directed fifteen episodes of *Star Trek;* in fact, after the two pilots were done, while we were all waiting to see if the network picked it up, Daniels directed Leonard in an episode of *Gunsmoke* called "The Treasure of John Walking Fox," in which once again Leonard played an enigmatic Native American.

D'Agosta also cast several other actors who appeared in episodes of *The Lieutenant* in *Star Trek,* including Walter Koenig and Nichelle Nichols, whom he'd discovered in an acting workshop. Actually, *The Lieutenant* episode in which Nichelle appeared was never broadcast, but perhaps more than any other episode in this series, it demonstrated what Gene Roddenberry intended to do with *Star Trek.*

Gene Roddenberry had a quiet vision of what television could be at its finest. He understood the impact it could have on society, but he had to spend a lot of time trying to sneak his social message past studio executives and the censors. This episode, entitled "To Set It Right," was shot while America was in the midst of the civil rights movement. Nichelle Nichols played the girlfriend of a white Marine, and Dennis Hopper played a Marine who objected to white men dating black women. It was a very controversial subject, and NBC decided it was too controversial to put on the air. I've spent considerable time with network executives. They think in bottom-line numbers, so it would be fascinating to have heard the discussions that must have taken place. It was extraordinary for a network to absorb the cost of producing an hour-long show and not broadcast it. The pressure from affiliate stations in different parts of the country must have been enormous. Knowing Roddenberry, I suspect he fought hard for this show, and though he lost the battle, he kept fighting his war. Setting *Star Trek* three hundred years in the future allowed him to focus on the social issues of the 1960s without being direct or obvious. The fact we were doing future fiction enabled him to film the first interracial kiss in American television history, when Captain Kirk is forced through telekinesis to passionately kiss Nichols's communications officer Lieutenant Uhura. The fact that Kirk had no control of his actions is demonstrated by the fact that Spock sings, dances, laughs, and also shares a passionate kiss with Barrett's Nurse Chapel, so clearly none of the crew members were acting of their own free will. Kirk was forced to kiss the beautiful Uhura!

Clearly that was fiction on many levels.

Joe D'Agosta was responsible for Leonard being cast in the role of Mr. Spock. Although D'Agosta was working at another studio when the *Star Trek* pilot was being cast, Roddenberry was unhappy with the actors he was seeing and asked him to help. He wasn't paid, although Roddenberry sent him a check for $750 when the series was picked up. "When I told Gene I didn't have time to do the casting," D'Agosta remembered, "he told me to just give him a list of names, and they would bring them in and make their deals through business affairs."

Roddenberry provided D'Agosta with a ten-page document that included only some broad character outlines. "There wasn't a lot of description of Spock in the script other than he was a half-human, half-alien Martian," he continued. "But what Gene wanted was a tall, lean Lincoln-ish character, who conveyed a sense of serenity. He had more of a physical image than a personality in his mind. He wanted an actor whose mostly humanlike appearance conveyed that he was a man of few words but had firm conclusions and thoughts. He was looking for someone who appeared to radiate a higher level of intelligence. Leonard fit that physical description but also projected that aura of intelligence. I eventually recommended three or four actors to Gene Roddenberry, and Leonard was one of them."

In Roddenberry's original outline, Spock was an alien member of the crew of the spaceship USS *Yorktown,* serving under Captain Robert April, as it traveled throughout the universe trying to offer assistance to civilizations in need. While Roddenberry always described it as the successful western series *Wagon Train* in space, for me it was more like the novelistic adventures of

Captain Horatio Hornblower in space. There certainly wasn't anything quite like it at the time. The audience loved westerns and detective shows; the only science fiction was being done on episodes of anthology series like *The Twilight Zone* and *The Outer Limits.*

Richard Arnold, the acknowledged expert of *Star Trek* who worked on several of the movies and TV shows, as well as organizing conventions, knew Roddenberry well. "*Star Trek* was a chance for him to tell the kind of stories he desperately wanted to tell. The timing was perfect because we were in the middle of the Cold War and the nuclear scare. He got his chance to do it in a science-fiction series because it went right over the heads of the censors. They didn't get it. He'd distracted their attention with a female character looking too sexy while telling stories about Vietnam, about sexual equality and racial issues, subjects you were not allowed to touch. Normally the censors would cross that all out, but because Gene used to say it all took place on purple planets with polka-dot people, they simply didn't get it. The role of Spock was pivotal; he was to be the representative of an intelligent society." In fact, in later interviews, Roddenberry described him as "the conscience of *Star Trek*."

There had never been a character quite like Mr. Spock. In most movie or TV portrayals, aliens from other planets were monsters either in being or deed, but whatever they were doing, it turned out to be bad for Earth. Spock was unique. Gene Roddenberry was creating a truly interracial and interspecies crew for the *Enterprise.* And Spock was half-human and half-alien, meaning he wasn't completely comfortable in two worlds. He actually wasn't identified as a Vulcan until the fifth or sixth episode. But the real function of Spock was to serve as an observer of human behavior and to comment on human variables, tendencies, habits, and beliefs. He was to be unfettered by normal human emotions.

Leonard learned he was being considered for a leading role in some new space show from his agent, who told him Roddenberry had liked his work on *The Lieutenant* and had him in mind for a character on a science-fiction series in development. I have no doubt how Leonard reacted; this was the kind of call agents make to clients to reassure them they are out there pounding the pavement on their behalf. While he must have been flattered, as apparently this was the first time he was considered for a leading role in a network series, he probably didn't take it very seriously. Calls like this one, and today e-mails, happen quite often in the life of a working actor. No one gets excited about them. It wasn't as if Leonard realized that this was going to be his big break and so fought to get the job. Sometimes these calls go a few steps further, but only rarely do they even progress to an audition, much less being cast in the role. I'm sure Leonard dismissed it before even hanging up the phone: a producer who was developing a pilot that might never get shot had him in mind for a role he might never get. Even if he got the role and the pilot was made, it had only a small chance of being picked up by the network.

But several weeks later, Brewis informed him that Roddenberry wanted to see other work he'd done to get a sense of his range. Leonard sent him an episode of *Dr. Kildare* in which he'd played a shy, sensitive character who befriended a blind girl and read poetry to her. It was pretty much the exact opposite of the brash producer he'd played on *The Lieutenant.* It turned out Roddenberry actually had seen that episode of *Kildare* but hadn't realized that was Leonard. Impressed, he invited Leonard to a meeting. "I went to that meeting expecting to audition for him," Leonard remembered. "Instead, he suggested we take a walk. We went to the scenic design department, and he showed me the sets and introduced me to the designers. We walked over to the prop department, and I saw some of the props being made. We went to wardrobe, and I began to realize this is interesting; it's like he's selling me on doing this job. I thought, you know what, if I keep my mouth shut, I might have a job here."

Roddenberry hadn't yet fully developed Spock in his own mind. As Leonard explained, "The best thing Gene Roddenberry gave to me when he offered me the part was to tell me that this character would have an internal struggle." The one thing that Roddenberry was adamant about was that the crew of this gigantic spaceship roaming through the universe would be an example of diversity. At a time when television was pretty much lily-white and all-American, Gene created a crew consisting of both men and women, people of color, different ethnic groups, and even a Russian to suggest the Cold War had ended. So he insisted Spock be obviously extraterrestrial; he wanted to make it clear that Spock came from another world and that these voyages were taking place far in the future, when interplanetary travel was common. That was the importance of the large, pointed ears.

What Leonard did not know until many years later was that Roddenberry already had decided that he wanted him to create the role of Mr. Spock. Dorothy C. Fontana, who had written the episode of *The Tall Man* in which Leonard appeared, was working as Roddenberry's production assistant. As she recalled, "I asked Gene, 'Who plays Spock?' And in response he slid a picture of Leonard across his desk at me."

The question was, who was going to play Captain Christopher Pike opposite him? Lloyd Bridges, James Coburn, Patrick O'Neal, and Jeffrey Hunter were all considered, but Hunter, who had appeared in numerous television series and movies — although he had played Jesus Christ in the movie *King of Kings* — got the part. In the first pilot episode, entitled "The Cage," Captain Pike is lured to a planet by a society with an amazing ability to, as Dr. Boyce, who would be replaced by Bones, explains, "create illusions out of a person's own thoughts, memories, and experiences, even out of a person's own desires — illusions just as real and solid as this tabletop and just as impossible to ignore." Their intent is to mate him to and produce children with a deformed human female who had crash-landed there. To make it incredibly difficult for Pike to resist, they transform this survivor into the women of his deepest desires.

Even in that initial voyage of the *Enterprise,* Roddenberry was using futuristic societies to tell relevant stories. In the pilot, one of the aliens lays out the simple rule that would govern many of the planets the crew would visit, as well as the communist nations then existing on Earth: "Wrong thinking is punishable; right thinking will be as quickly rewarded. You will find it an effective combination."

It was the most expensive pilot NBC had ever produced, and the network didn't like it. Basically, it was too intellectual, and there was not enough action. But the executives still liked Roddenberry's concept and made the almost unheard-of decision to make a second pilot. This is where I came in. I've been told that Jeffrey Hunter's wife started making extraordinary demands, and as a result, Roddenberry fired him. The first choice to replace him was Jack Lord, who asked for 50 percent ownership of the show. That's when Roddenberry called me. I've never known why he offered the role to me. Perhaps it was because I'd played leading roles in several major TV series. I'd played major roles in several motion pictures, including *Judgment at Nuremberg* and *Incubus,* the first motion picture made entirely in the universal language of Esperanto.

Or, it also might have been that he was getting desperate, I was available, and I was the right type. Leonard was dark and brooding; I was blond and bright-eyed. Leonard displayed little emotion; I was a walking mood ring. As I have often explained to audiences at *Star Trek* conventions, I suspect Roddenberry felt I was the perfect choice for the lead role in a show because I wasn't too intelligent for the audience and he didn't have to pay me a lot of money.

I was in a New York hotel room when he called. I had just finished doing a legal series called *For the People.* He explained that he'd made a pilot for a science-fiction show called *Star Trek,* and NBC hadn't bought it, but they liked the project enough to make a second pilot with a different cast.

He asked me to come to Los Angeles to see it, with the idea of playing the captain. I don't remember his precise words, but I presume he'd said something like, "It's the leading man. He gets the girl. He fights the villains. He runs, and he jumps. And he gets first billing." However, I am quite certain during that first conversation he did not mention that I would be playing against a half-man, half-alien with, as Leonard later described them, "Dumbo ears."

I thought the pilot was magical, and even with all its problems, the potential was obvious. These many years later, after all the amazing space movies and special effects that have made us all feel as if we are in space, it's absolutely impossible to accurately convey how innovative this concept was at that time. These were normal people hundreds of years in the future, and when they weren't otherwise occupied saving the universe and their own lives, they were dealing with the same issues and relationship problems the audience dealt with every day. But after viewing that pilot, I told Roddenberry I thought the characters were taking themselves much too seriously. Every line seemed meaningful. There was no sense of fun or playfulness. The characters seemed to be talking at each other rather than relating to each other. Ironically, just about the only person who smiled in the entire episode was Spock.

Roddenberry agreed with me and offered me the role of James Tiberius Kirk.

A lot of changes were made before the second pilot was shot. As *Variety* reported on November 5, 1965, the only two members of the original cast to be retained, Majel Barrett and Leonard Nimoy, had been signed for the pilot of "an hourlong color science fiction adventure series to be produced by Desilu for NBC." That brief item actually was wrong — the series was shot in black and white. When that item appeared, Leonard was doing exactly what an actor should be doing — working. He was co-starring with the beautiful Juliet Prowse in a Valley Musical Theater production of the show *Irma la Douce.*

In addition to a new script in which Barrett's role was reduced and replaced by a relationship between Spock and Kirk, fundamental changes were made to the character of Mr. Spock. Spock was the result of all the work Leonard had done in his career. While he made Spock so realistic, it was easy to believe he was based on a living being; in fact, he started from very little. Because Leonard did such a remarkable job bringing Spock to life, I'm not sure he ever got all the credit he deserved for the creation of this iconic character. As Joe D'Agosta remembered, "Spock was not on that page. The whole character, other than the physicality that was described by Gene, was created by Leonard. He embodied that character with its essence."

But initially, at least, Leonard hadn't gotten a good hold on the character; he was experimenting to see what fit. After that first pilot, Spock never smiled again. "I knew it was a mistake after the fact," Leonard told me. "When I saw it, I thought it destroyed the mystique. It destroyed the design of this person. This person smiling is not appropriate. This person is not necessarily a negative or dour person, but this person is not a frivolous person. This person must be played as a scientist and a student of what's going on."

The appearance of Spock also continued to evolve. Initially, when the show was going to be in color, Fred Phillips, who did his makeup, tinted his skin a reddish color. It was supposed to suggest a Martian heritage. But when it was tested on black-and-white sets, it just looked black. The character was not a black person. So Fred substituted a Max Factor makeup called "Chinese Yellow," which gave Spock's skin a slightly yellowish tone. It was enough to emphasize that he wasn't Caucasian, but much better than the Martian red.

Leonard initially thought Spock should have a crude look, with a jagged haircut and bushy eyebrows. He had his eyebrows shaved and then drawn in. But Spock's quite-famous ears always were an issue. Roddenberry wanted him to have pointed ears, which instantly would inform viewers that he was from another planet. Leonard had some trepidation about those ears, wondering if they looked too comical. But Roddenberry insisted on it. The studio contracted a company to produce the original prosthetic ear pieces, and they were terrible. "Grotesque and funny," Leonard called them. It took some time and a lot of effort before he was satisfied.

There continued to be considerable debate about Spock's appearance. After we shot the second pilot and NBC picked it up, the publicity department began promoting it. One afternoon, Leonard got a copy of the brochure announcing the show in the mail. It was taking place in the twenty-third century, would go where no man had gone before, blah, blah, blah. It included photographs of members of the cast. But when Leonard looked at Spock, something seemed not quite right. As he looked closely, he realized that the photo had been altered; Spock's curved eyebrows had been straightened, and the pointed tips at the ends of his ears had been removed. Leonard's reaction was to feel threatened. He wondered if these changes meant they weren't satisfied with the character. As he said, this was going to be the first steady acting job he'd ever had, the first time a job had lasted more than two weeks. He called Roddenberry, who admitted he was getting pushback about the character from the sales department. They were concerned about a number of issues but primarily that the ears looked devilish, which they believed would make it difficult to sell the show in the Bible Belt. They didn't believe those people would welcome a character that reminded them of the devil into their homes each week. Roddenberry reassured him that Spock was an essential element of the show. Those ears, which took hours to put on each morning, eventually became the most defining feature of the character. Leonard loved to tell a story about the night he attended a promotion party on the Paramount lot; he was sitting in his chair when suddenly he felt two large hands squeezing his shoulders from behind, and then he heard the instantly identifiable voice of John Wayne whispering in his real ear, "I recognize you. You had your ears fixed!"

The second script added more dimension to the character, and it was gradually becoming clear that Spock would be more intellectual than reactive. That he would be controlled and logical rather than emotional. The precedent for that character was created by Michael Rennie in the 1951 movie *The Day the Earth Stood Still*. Rennie played an alien who came to Earth to warn against moving forward into the atomic age. The character was extremely intelligent and totally detached, rational, cool, and peaceful.

To better understand the core of that character, as Leonard had been trained to do, he looked into his own life. Spock wasn't simply an alien — he was alienated; the product of two very different civilizations, he didn't fit comfortably anywhere. Leonard drew on his own experience growing up in Boston, explaining, "I knew what it meant to be a member of a minority, in some instances an outcast minority. I understood that aspect of the character well enough to play it. Coming from my background, growing up in a neighborhood of immigrants trying to assimilate into modern American society, believe me, I understood that deep sense of not really belonging anywhere."

Leonard liked to tell people that he had been born in Boston, his parents had come to America as immigrants, aliens, and then he went to Hollywood to become an alien.

If there was a character that he drew on to create the sense of alienation he needed, it probably came from one of his favorite movies, *The Hunchback of Notre Dame,* in which the great Charles Laughton created the unforgettable Quasimodo. Quasimodo was the essential outsider, and Leonard had so much empathy for him that he wanted to cry when he saw that movie. He wanted the audience to empathize with Spock, who was caught in an internal struggle between his human side and his Vulcan side, which resulted in a continuous struggle between logic and emotion. "I knew that we weren't playing a man with no emotions," he once said, "but rather a man who had great pride, who had learned to control his emotions, and who would deny what those emotions were.

"In spite of being an outcast, being mixed up, looking different, he maintains his point of view. He can't be bullied or put on. He's freaky with dignity. There are very few characters who have that kind of pride, cool, and ability to lay it out and walk away."

Spock was the result of seventeen years of being kicked around but remaining dedicated and respectful to the craft.

Ironically, a lot of the character's movements also came from an unlikely source.

In the 1950s, Leonard went to the Greek Theatre, a famed Los Angeles amphitheater, to see the great Harry Belafonte perform. The stage was dark. A single spotlight suddenly focused on Belafonte standing alone, his hands on his thighs, slightly hunched. He received a big ovation, which he did not acknowledge, then began singing. When the sound ended again, there was huge applause. Belafonte still didn't respond; he simply began singing his second song. "He must have been on stage for ten or fifteen minutes before making a gesture," Leonard recalled. "And then, in the middle of a song, he simply raised his arm. It was gigantic because it came from a very minimal place. The theater exploded with a roar in response. The whole place shook. Wow, what a lesson that was. If you are minimal, then even a small gesture becomes a big deal. I learned a lot from that."

James T. Kirk was considerably easier to develop because it was a familiar character in American culture. He was the square-jawed hero running into the abyss to save the damsel in distress. In fact, joining the cast so late in development, I had to rely at least somewhat on the lines that I was given to define my character. I was so concerned with learning my lines, getting them out, becoming comfortable with the set, and my relationship with the other members of my crew that I didn't have the opportunity to look deep in Jim Kirk's psyche. For the first few weeks, at least, I was feasting on my own narcissism, as actors will do, because I was mostly fighting for survival.

Everyone attached to the production in that initial stage had his or her own concerns. The only person concerned solely about my part was me. It was my complete focus. It becomes the bone the dog is guarding, and the longer it goes, the more ferocious the dog guarding it becomes. That led me into a tunneled point of view on the creation of Kirk.

It took me a while to take what Leonard and later DeForest Kelley were doing with their characters and amplify it through James T. Kirk.

I have no memory of meeting Leonard on the set. I'm sure we were polite. I suspect we shook hands firmly. One of us might have even made a little joke about the adventure on which we were about to embark. But both of us — all of the actors — had done so much television by this time that we had been through the meeting and greeting numerous times. On occasion, there would be an actor whom we'd worked with before and we'd spend a few minutes catching up, but in this case, I didn't know anyone in the cast. I doubt either Leonard or I even realized we'd worked together previously in *U.N.C.L.E.* That's just the nature of our profession.

There actually was probably more pressure on me than anyone else when we started. The first pilot had failed. Roddenberry was being given a second — and last — chance to create the future. I had starred on Broadway. I had starred in movies. I had been the lead in a previous television series. I was asked to do the role of Captain Kirk. I didn't audition like everyone else did, so ostensibly, I was the star of *Star Trek.* I got top billing, and if the show failed, the message would be *Shatner can't carry a show.*

I don't know what was going on in Leonard's mind. I think what goes through the actor's mind is simply, *I've got a good role here, it looks like the show is going to go, and I've got to play this role as best I can.* At this point in his career, Leonard was an experienced professional actor, although he hadn't played leading roles. He had always been a supporting actor, often playing a bad guy or an ethnic character. At the beginning, I suspect the concept of wearing pointed ears and a blunt haircut might have seemed a bit bizarre to him. If it had been me, I know I would have been thinking, *I'd like to get rid of these ears and appear more normal.*

As the actor who spent considerable time looking directly at Spock, believe me, those ears were noticeable. Eventually, time — and Leonard's commitment to the part — made them seem somewhat normal.

Leonard did tell me years later one of his goals for this part: in all his other roles, his name had been written on his dressing room door — when he did have his own dressing room — in chalk. Just once he wanted to see his name painted on the dressing room door.

The second pilot episode was entitled "Where No Man Has Gone Before." Basically, the plot involves the *Enterprise* and her crew being threatened by crew members who develop malevolent psychic powers after the ship passes through an invisible barrier.

The very first scene we shot took place on the *Enterprise*'s bridge. As George Takei remembered it, "Leonard and Bill, Jimmy Doohan were there, Paul Fix, playing our doctor, and I came on board. Nichelle Nichols was not in this episode, but Sally Kellerman was. In that first scene, we were all trying to work with this new set. People were figuring out how to move, how to touch, how to sit, and Leonard was very calculated in everything that he did. He was trying to figure out how a being of superintelligence and logic would move or touch the buttons. He was finding out how he would relate to his console, how he would move from the console down the steps to the lower deck, to the captain's chair and navigation console. He didn't just move; he planned every step in character.

"Then we began to discuss the scene. What I found fascinating about Leonard was that, while the other actors had our lines memorized and were just going to go through it, he wanted to question and discuss everything before the scene began. He asked endless questions. He was a very thoughtful and analytical actor. He needed to understand why he was doing what he was doing. It took tremendous preparation to make what he did seem so natural.

"I was impressed by that, and I did the same thing. I made every button specific for me."

From the very beginning, Leonard and I worked together easily. I approached a scene very differently from the way he did. When the scene began, I was where the director needed me to be, and if the director was any good, he'd let the actors feel it out. While Leonard would plan the entire scene, I just let things happen, delivering my lines in a manner that would be commensurate with what people were doing. If Leonard stayed at his station, for example, because he felt that was where Spock was most comfortable, then Kirk would go to him. I would move over to him or either sit or stand in response to what he was doing. He had to play unemotional, so for me, that was a great part of the challenge, playing against someone who wasn't showing any emotion.

Leonard had to learn how to work with me too. He told me once, "There was a significant difference between my playing against Jeffrey Hunter and playing against you. One of the reasons for the shift in Spock's character was that you came on board. Jeffrey Hunter was a very internalized actor. A fine actor, an intelligent man. This was the way he worked: he was very internalized, very thoughtful. There's an old joke about two actors trying to play a scene. One asks the other, 'What are you going to play in this scene?'

"And that actor says, 'I'm playing nothing.'

"Then the first actor says, 'No, no, no.

You can't play nothing. I'm playing nothing!' So with Jeffrey Hunter I felt the need to help drive the action. Otherwise, we're both playing nothing. When you came on board with your energy, and a sense of humor, and a twinkle in the eye, I was able to become the core Spock." Then he added, "And I never smiled again."

From the very beginning, Leonard fought to bring a real sense of dignity to Spock. While other actors might have chosen to play the character with the type of whimsy normally associated with Spock's pointed-ear appearance, he took everything Spock did absolutely seriously. Nothing was silly or frivolous. While we've seen others bring characters like this to life since then, especially with franchises like *Star Wars,* Leonard proved it could be done.

It wasn't always easy. Several weeks before the show went on the air, NBC had us doing promotion. It was a typical publicity event: groups of reporters moved from one character to the next, asking the same questions over and over. They asked questions like: What's the show about? What can you tell us about the character you play? What planet is he from? Does he really have pointed ears?

"We're doing real stories," Leonard responded. "We're doing stories about over-population. We're doing stories about racial issues. We're doing stories about ecology, about loyalty and brotherhood." Spock, he explained, was a fascinating character. He was very intelligent, and he had great dignity. Spock was a scientist, he continued, emphasizing the fact that this was not your typical alien character, and any preconceptions the media had based on all the science-fiction stories that had come before really didn't apply.

The next day, the reporters were invited onto the soundstage to watch us film a scene. It was an opportunity for Leonard to demonstrate his commitment to the integrity of the character. Unfortunately, this particular scene took place in the sick bay. Spock had been seriously wounded in a fight. As Kirk rushes in, Spock is lying on a bed, bright-green blood dripping from his foot. "What happened, Spock?" Kirk demands.

"Captain," he responds with as much dignity as he can muster, "a monster attacked me!"

Obviously, I didn't have to fight the same battles for dignity, because Kirk actually was fighting battles. As it quickly developed, Spock was the mind of the show; DeForest

Kelley, who joined the cast as Dr. Leonard "Bones" McCoy was the heart; and I was the action hero. Captain Kirk was the classic warrior, leading his men into battle against great odds to emerge battered and bruised but victorious.

And then we went on the air.

# FOUR

Unlike the enigmatic Spock, Leonard was a man of many passions. Among those things that fascinated him was the artist Vincent van Gogh. He wrote and starred in a one-man show, *Vincent,* based on the letters between Vincent and his brother Theo. Actor Jean-Michel Richaud, who followed Leonard in the role and actually brought it to France, spent considerable time with Leonard talking about Van Gogh. As Richaud told me, Leonard "was intrigued by Van Gogh's uncompromising attitude toward the work. In Van Gogh's day, people equated art with commerce, and very much it mirrors what we see today. We talked about that struggle between art and commerce. Leonard embraced his success, and used it to support the arts.

"But we also talked at length about how Vincent believed 'there is nothing more truly artistic than to love people.' The bottom line of this play was about love; it wasn't about the crazy person that everybody thinks Vincent was. It was about love for art, love for his brother, love for the truth. To me, that was the common point between Vincent and Leonard, both of them were seekers of truth in art."

Van Gogh also said of friendship, "Close friends are truly life's treasures. Sometimes they know us better than we know ourselves. With gentle honesty, they are there to guide and support us, to share our laughter and our tears. Their presence reminds us that we are never really alone."

My own life has moved constantly at such a rapid pace and is usually filled with so many people that I rarely take the time to wonder why I have had so many wonderful acquaintances but so very few real friends. It must be some quirk in my own character. But I was somewhat painfully reminded of that early in 2015 when I participated in an eight-day cross-country motorcycle ride from Chicago to Los Angeles. It was a difficult trip through some extraordinary heat; I fainted twice. Among the riders were two sets of brothers. Carl and Kevin were among the organizers of this trip; they were four years apart in age. Kevin had asked his brother to ride with us because it would give them at least a little time to spend together that they rarely had. About halfway through the trip, Carl had to leave to fulfill other commitments. As he left, they hugged each other and wept. Grown men in their fifties weeping at losing the chance to spend more time together. I was struck by their love for each other.

The other set of brothers, another Kevin and his brother, Brian, were thirteen months apart. They rode side by side, loving each other, backing each other, each describing his brother as his best friend. They also had fights, one night they described choking each other, but the next morning, whatever caused that was gone. They love each other, and they are each other's best friend. That is something that is very rare, very enviable, and, to me, something that must be cherished when achieved. And for a time, I had that with Leonard, and I lost it.

We certainly didn't start our journey as close friends. Rather, like the other members of our cast, we were colleagues, feeling each other out, learning our professional strengths and weaknesses and trying to bring our A game to the show. The friendships that developed initially were in the scripts: the relationship between Kirk and Spock held the show together. The two of us were on-screen in almost every scene. Leonard described the relationship between these two characters as a "great sense of brotherhood. Spock was tremendously loyal and had a great appreciation for the talent and the leadership abilities of Kirk. He was totally devoted to seeing to it that whatever Kirk needed to be done got done."

Conversely, Kirk relied on Spock unfailingly for his advice, knowing it would never be encumbered by any thoughts of personal gain or tempered by emotional constraints. But he also depended on him to share the burdens of command. With the exception of Dee Kelley's McCoy, Kirk had to maintain the distance of command from the rest of the crew. That can be a lonely place if there is no outlet, and Spock provided that outlet for Kirk.

It was clear to me from the first scene we did together that Leonard was a fine actor and that he was completely invested in the part. He gave us a living, breathing character to work with, rather than forcing us to play against a comic-book cliché. The fact that he took this pointed-eared alien so seriously forced the rest of us to do so with our characters as well.

That sense of professionalism also was true of pretty much everyone else in the cast. Gene Roddenberry had put together a talented, experienced company. Everyone showed up on time in the morning, well prepared, and we got our work done, then went our separate ways at the end of the day. While there was the usual camaraderie at first, there weren't any friendships developing. That's the nature of our business.

Even after we had completed the pilot and had gotten picked up, there was no guarantee of success. The majority of television programs fail quickly. Actors live forever on the edge of failure: every play will close, every show will go off the air. At least that's what we all believed. Failure on some level will come; it is only a question of how long it can be delayed.

Dorothy Fontana remembers the very first hint she got that the show was going to be successful. At 9:00 A.M. the morning after our first episode, her phone rang. A recognizable voice explained, "This is Leslie Nielsen." Leslie Nielsen had starred in the classic science-fiction film *Forbidden Planet.* When Fontana explained that Gene Roddenberry hadn't arrived yet, Nielsen said, "I just wanted to let him know that I saw the show last night, and I think it has a great future." Then the mail started arriving. The first week there was one bag of mail. People were writing that they loved the show and asked for autographed pictures. That was encouraging. The second week we got three bags of mail. That was interesting. And then the deluge started, and in fact, it still hasn't ended. We had not the slightest idea what we were creating; we were always fighting to stay on the air one more season, one more week.

Gene Roddenberry had not been satisfied with the first episode. In fact, he liked to tell people that after that first show aired, his father had gone up and down the block in his neighborhood apologizing for it. But a week later, Roddenberry was having lunch in a restaurant near the studio when he overheard people excitedly discussing the previous night's episode. That was the first time he'd ever heard people talking about one of his shows, so he thought, *This might be something special.*

What was surprising to me was that rather than Captain James T. Kirk, the character who received the most attention, and the most fan mail, was Mr. Spock. This was long before Leonard and I became friends, and honestly, I hadn't expected it, and I was not especially thrilled about it. I was being paid the largest salary, I was out front for the publicity, I had the most lines, my character's fate carried the storyline, my character got the girl and saved the ship. The natural flow of events should have been that Kirk would receive the most attention, not some alien with strange-looking ears. But the spectacular performance Leonard gave occupied all that attention in the beginning. Mr. Spock fan clubs were formed. Newspapers and magazines ran features on this extraordinary new character. Roddenberry got a memo from the network suggesting that Spock be featured in every story. My future was on the line, and that line seemed to be getting shaky. And so, for a few weeks, I was quite jealous. It bothered me so much that I went to Roddenberry's office to discuss it with him. Gene was the voice of good reason in this case. "Don't be afraid of having other popular and talented people around you," he said. "They can only enhance your performance. The more you work with these people, the better the show is going to be." In other words, the more popular Spock became, the better it was for everyone, including me, and I settled down to that lovely fact.

Spock continued to evolve as Leonard explored all the possibilities of the character. It was a considerably more complex task than usual because there were no recognizable hallmarks. This was a brand-new character in American culture; he was carving out the path. There was no traditional right or wrong; the audience would tell him what was true. So Leonard took great care to protect Spock. "Characters have to depend on the kindness of actors," he once explained. "I felt particularly that way with Spock because I think Spock could easily become cartoonish or silly. Liberties could be taken, and I had to prevent that."

Bringing Spock to life probably was the most difficult role of his career. And he admitted to having some concern that he wouldn't be taken seriously as an actor. At first, he was worried that the whole show was a foolish enterprise, and he would be known forever for wearing devilish ears and playing an alien on a spaceship. He was right about that, and in less competent hands, it could have become a very campy show and been embarrassing for all of us.

But that never happened, and certainly part of the reason was that we all approached it seriously. We knew our audience would take the show only as seriously as we did. To get to the core Spock, as he once explained to an interviewer, "I went through the process of gradually internalizing more and more and more. There were

117

times that I had to remind myself of that because that wasn't my nature. On the contrary, my training as an actor was to use my emotions, to use gesture, to use color in my speech, to use tonalities to be interesting. And to be passionate. I always enjoyed playing passionate characters, so this was quite a shift for me. It wasn't me at all. It became me."

Perhaps Roddenberry had known more than we suspected when he cast me in the role of Kirk, because it turned out that our differing approaches to our parts resulted in perfect harmony. Leonard explained it better than I would: "Shatner was energy personified. A ball of energy, constantly looking, digging, searching, which gave me a place to exist as Spock. Much more so, with all due respect, to Jeff Hunter. Jeff Hunter played Captain Pike as a thoughtful, more introverted person. My tendency, when I was in a scene with him, was to try to be more energetic around him. Bill Shatner provided all the energy you needed in the scene, allowing me to be more reflective and more reactive. The fact that Shatner came on the way he did, I think it helped me a lot in developing the Spock character."

As the weeks passed and Leonard became more comfortable in the role, he became very protective of Spock. Next to playing Spock, writing his part had to be the most difficult. The crux of great drama is the expression of emotion; just imagine how difficult it was for the writers to bring to life a character whose most identifiable character trait was that he did not express emotion. "We couldn't let him show emotion," remembered Dorothy Fontana, or D. C. Fontana as she became known. While she personally wrote several episodes, she also worked with the other writers the entire run of the show and knew how hard it was to write for that character. "Since he was half-human, there were moments when we had to let him show something. We had to let something leak through." One device the writers used several times was creating some sort of mind control that the enemy used to force Spock to display an emotion — once it even was love. As long as the script was logical, Leonard clearly enjoyed the opportunity to explore his character. And while Leonard remembered being a pain in the neck for the writers with all his script notes, claiming he was very often highly critical, no one I've spoken with actually remembers that to be true. Dorothy Fontana doesn't recall that, and I can't remember a situation until much, much later, when we were making the movies, that he became overly protective of Spock.

Only once during the original series was there a real issue. The head writer for the show was Gene Coon. It was Gene Coon who created the Klingons, an irrational race of warriors who believed in nothing but conquest and would destroy anything and anyone that got in their way. The Klingons were the perfect enemy. During that first season, we were given a script in which Spock did something he hadn't done before; I don't remember what it was, but Leonard felt it was completely inconsistent with what he had been developing for the character. As he had been throughout his career, he focused on small details that others might have overlooked. So he went to Coon's office to discuss it.

Coon was in the middle of the next script. The last thing he needed was an actor fussing over a detail that no one would notice. Leonard explained to him why the scene didn't work. Apparently, Coon listened carefully, then suggested, "Just do it."

"I can't," Leonard told him, an actor being protective of his character.

"This conversation's over," Coon snapped.

By the time Leonard returned to the set,

his agent was on the phone telling him he was being suspended. As he remembered the incident, "I knew it couldn't possibly lead to them telling me not to come to work anymore, because this was a machine, and if you pull a cog out, the machine stops. So in my arrogance, I said to my agent, 'Ask them do I have to finish the day, or can I leave now?' "

The next call came from Roddenberry, who quickly dismissed the suspension and brought everybody into his office. Leonard had great respect for Coon — we all did — but protecting Spock was far more important to him. Coon made the requested changes, and Leonard went back to work.

Leonard remained adamant that the mythology we were creating had to be consistent and accurate throughout all our explorations. *Star Trek VI: The Undiscovered Country,* for example, included a scene in which Kirk and Spock were having dinner with the Klingons. In writer and director Nick Meyer's script, Spock had a line that stated the Federation and the Klingons had been at war for a period of time. He wasn't sure that was accurate and checked with our resident expert Richard Arnold, who confirmed that there had not been a war in that timeframe, and the line was changed to reflect that. Details mattered to Leonard. Once, when he was working on the western series *The Tall Man,* just before they started filming he took off his wedding ring and put it in a locked valuables box. When asked about that, he explained that men didn't wear wedding rings during that period. Who would know that? Who would take the time to find out? Leonard, that's who. He invested completely in the creation of a character, and all the work he had done all those years finally paid off when he got the opportunity to truly create a character.

He explained that to me once, "No one else is going to provide that consistency and continuity. If the writers gave me the line, 'Let's make hay under the Vulcan moon,' it was up to me to remind them that three episodes earlier Spock had mentioned that Vulcan had no moons."

Most of the hallmarks that became associated with Spock, in particular the Vulcan neck pinch and the Vulcan salute, were entirely his creation. In one of our first episodes, Kirk's personality was split into good and evil, and evil Kirk was about to kill good Kirk. In the script, Spock was supposed to sneak up behind evil Kirk and knock him out by hitting him over the head with the butt of his phaser. It was the kind of bad-guy move that Leonard had been doing for a long time. But while our scripts regularly required me to always be punching, rolling, jumping, swinging, butting heads, and getting hit in the face, this was the first time Spock actually participated in a physically violent action. Leonard wasn't comfortable with that; brawling, banging someone in the head somehow seemed below Spock's evolved personality. It was too twentieth century. So he suggested to the director that Spock had a special capability that allowed him to put enemies out of action without little physical exertion. The director was open to the concept. Leonard and I sat down, and he told me what he had in mind: he would pinch my trapezius muscle, and I would collapse in a heap. I have no idea where that concept came from, but I was a professional actor; I knew how to fall down. Of course, it fit Spock perfectly: an advanced civilization would know where the vital nerves are located and have the physical strength to take advantage of that knowledge to incapacitate their enemy. We did the scene: Spock came up behind evil Kirk and pinched his trapezius, I dropped to the floor, and the Vulcan nerve pinch was born.

For those people counting at home, fans

of the show saw the Vulcan nerve pinch being used thirty-four different times. I wonder how many kids since then have had to suffer through the real pain of a Vulcan neck pinch.

The Vulcan salute has become recognized literally throughout the world. In this salute, the right hand is held up with the pinkie and ring finger touching, but separated from the middle finger and forefinger, which also are touching, in a modified V-for-victory salute. It was created for the first episode of our second season, by which time Leonard had a strong understanding of Spock. In this episode, Spock has to return to Vulcan to fulfill a marriage betrothal that was arranged when he was a child. If he doesn't return, he will die. This episode was written by the great science-fiction writer Theodore Sturgeon. This is the first time we have seen Spock on Vulcan, among the people of his race. In the script, he is greeted by the woman who is to conduct the marriage ceremony. Leonard suggested to the director that there needed to be some type of Vulcan greeting that would be appropriate. It would be the Vulcan version of a handshake, a kiss, a nod or bow, or a military salute. When the director agreed, Leonard had to create it. It was not an especially easy thing to envision. It needed to be unlike any traditional greeting, but it couldn't be at all comical. As he often did, Leonard drew on his own life to find it.

There is a gesture he had first seen when he was eight years old, when he went with his grandfather, father, and brother to the North Russell Street shul, an Orthodox synagogue, and he had never forgotten it. In Jewish Orthodox tradition, during the benediction the Shechinah, which very roughly means the feminine counterpart to God, enters the sanctuary to bless the congregation. The Shechinah is so powerful that simply looking at it could cause serious or even fatal injury. So worshipers use this gesture, in which their fingers form the shape of the Hebrew letter *shin,* to hide their eyes. "I wasn't supposed to look," he remembered, "but I knew something major was happening. So I peeked." The gesture always intrigued him. "I didn't know what it meant for a long time," he said. "But it seemed magical to me, and I learned how to do it. There was no reason for me to learn it, but it looked like fun." Not only did he use it as the basis for the traditional Vulcan greeting in the episode, many years later he published a controversial book of naked glamorous women wearing religious symbols, entitled *Shekhina.*

The gesture immediately caught on. Fans of the show started greeting him with it on the street — without realizing they were blessing each other. Giving this greeting requires a certain dexterity. Not everybody can do it. Some of our actors had problems with it, and they had to use their other hand to put their fingers in place, then hold up their hand for the camera. Aside from me, another actor who had difficulty giving this gesture was Zachary Quinto, who years later played young Spock for the first time in the 2009 motion picture. While promoting the new film, he admitted to Leonard, "I spent a little time actually training my hands to be able to do the salute. That wasn't something that came particularly easy, so I would rubber band my ring finger and my pinkie finger together while I was driving around Los Angeles and do little exercises for months leading up to the shooting."

While Leonard was creating these elements, our writers were smart enough to recognize them as integral parts of the character and incorporate them into future scripts. I've often said that no one could do more with a raised eyebrow than Spock, but of course Spock had the strangest eyebrows. Leonard apparently had a habit of raising an eyebrow to emphasize his concern or his questioning of a statement or an action. It isn't that unusual. Maybe he had used this gesture on-screen before, but before, he didn't have such prominent eyebrows, and he wasn't getting full-face close-ups. So he did it naturally in one scene, and the following week, a script direction read: Spock lifts an eyebrow. That became another character trait; the writers loved it and had him raising an eyebrow in just about every episode until he insisted they stop.

Several of Spock's phrases also have become part of the general culture, but none of them are as widely known as the four words said when giving the Vulcan salute that have come to have such deep meaning: "Live long and prosper." They were written by Theodore Sturgeon for the same episode and are now known by the abbreviation LLAP — which was the way Leonard ended all his own tweets.

Spock also was associated with a unique, four-syllable pronunciation of the word, "fascinating," which often was reinforced by an arched eyebrow. It wasn't simply the word; it was the way he drew it out that gave it such meaning. It also was a good window into his talent as an actor. It's a simple word, we all know what it means, and there may be a thousand different ways of pronouncing it. But finding the one way to say it that reinforces the subtext of the character can be extremely difficult.

That word was used, he explained, to describe something unexpected, usually something that he had not seen before. It actually was a wonderful word to describe exploration into new worlds that didn't always adhere to the rules of science or, where Spock was concerned, logic. He always credited Spock's pronunciation to a director. In one of our early episodes, "The Corbomite Maneuver," we were all on the bridge gathered around a computer screen. Spock's reaction to what we were looking at was that one word, "Fascinating," but it was kind of flat. It didn't carry with it the awe that the director, Joe Sargent, wanted. So he told Leonard, "Be different. Be the scientist. See it as something that's a curiosity rather than a threat." He tried it several different ways until he got it just right, spoken in a detached tone of appreciation for something that exceeded his knowledge or expectations. As he said later about that moment, "A big chunk of the character was born right there."

It actually took me some time to fully understand Leonard's total commitment to

Spock, and that led to our first real fight. Not our only fight, just our first one. This took place during our first season, and we were all sort of feeling our way along. By then, the cast was complete: in addition to Leonard, Majel Barrett, and me, DeForest Kelley had come aboard to play Dr. "Bones" McCoy, James Doohan's chief engineer "Scotty" kept the ship running, our communications officer was Nichelle Nichols's Lieutenant Nyota Uhura, our helmsman was Lieutenant Hikaru Sulu as created by George Takei, and Walter Koenig was our bow to the Cold War then raging, the Russian-accented navigator Pavel Chekov. We were learning more about each other, and how to work together, each week. While we were being molded into a cast, we were all actors trying to further our own careers, so there was the usual competition. "A constant struggle to inject yourself," was how Leonard described it, "to try to find ways of making more of a contribution." It was no different from any other cast. "A family," he said, "in which everybody's looking for their position. How come he gets all the good food, and I get the leftovers . . . how come she's got the good potatoes, mine are cold."

While I was becoming comfortable with

the popularity of Spock, in those first few months, Leonard and I kept a respectful distance. We were always friendly, always polite, and absolutely always professional, but it wouldn't be accurate to write that a friendship was developing. We had a good professional, respectful relationship. One of the early episodes we did was called "The Devil in the Dark." For many people it remains one of their favorite episodes. The story began when the *Enterprise* visited a planet on which miners were being killed by a strange creature, which lived deep underground, known as a Horta. The Horta had no means of communicating with humans, so to understand its motives, Spock had to "mind meld" with it, a technique that allowed a Vulcan to merge his or her mind what that of another living being. This was known to be a difficult, dangerous, and very painful process in which the Vulcan actually feels the intense pain of the mind-melding counterpart. Spock endured that pain to discover that this otherwise harmless creature was the last of its race and simply was protecting its eggs from the miners' intrusion. With that knowledge, Kirk was able to forge a peaceful working relationship between the humans and the Horta.

It was a wonderful script, but it included no instruction about how to mind meld, which left it up to Leonard to create the action. I figured the mind meld would be something like a radio signal, in which invisible waves traveled between two people. But when I asked him how he intended to do it, I can vividly remember him placing his forefinger and thumb on my forehead and explaining, "Here's how we would do it." It was more like cable than wireless, a physical rather than a mental connection.

We were filming that episode when I was informed that my father had died suddenly of a massive heart attack while playing golf in Florida. I was utterly and totally devastated; I was shaken to the core of my soul both physically and emotionally. I had to go to Florida as quickly as I could get there, but there was no flight for several hours. We were in the middle of a scene, and I decided it was important to continue working. The only way I knew to escape the pain I was feeling was to become someone else, and so I slipped into the guise of James T. Kirk. I owed that to my fellow actors.

Those were the most difficult moments I've ever spent on a soundstage. I tried to blank out everything except the persona of my character but had only limited success.

When we'd rehearsed in the morning, I'd known my lines, I was a professional, and I was always prepared; but when we resumed work in the afternoon, I stumbled and had great difficulty remembering those lines. Years later, when Leonard and I discussed it, I recalled being stoic, but his memory was different. He told me I continued to repeat, as if in a daze, "Promises not kept. Promises not kept. Things that he wanted to do."

While I was in the midst of true emotional pain, Leonard was enacting the pain caused by mind melding. He got on his hands and knees, placed his hands on the Horta, and cried, "Pain, pain, pain . . ." It's a tricky scene for an actor to pull off without looking very silly, but Leonard had created an aura of believability around Spock, and he was able to make it work.

In that scene, Kirk has to react to Spock's pain. I returned to the set several days later, after burying my father. The first thing we shot were close-ups of my reaction. The entire cast had been truly sympathetic about my loss, and it was a hard day for all of us. There was a lot of tension on the set, and I wanted to find a way of showing everyone that I was okay. While preparing to do my scenes, I'd looked at the footage of Spock mind melding with the Horta, and Leonard graciously offered to work with me. "Show me what you did," I said.

"Well, I went over here and put my hands on her and cried, 'Pain, pain, pain.' "

Having watched the footage, I knew it was far more emotional than that. I asked him to show me exactly what he did.

Leonard got down on his hands and knees, closed his eyes, and reenacted the scene to give me something to react to. He didn't simply rush through it, he felt the emotion. He screamed out from the depths of his soul, "Pain . . . pain . . . pain . . ."

Rather than respecting his commitment to the work, I went for the cheap joke. I called out, "Can somebody get this guy an aspirin?" I waited for a laugh that never came. Leonard was furious, absolutely furious. I could see the anger in his face. He thought I'd set him up for ridicule, then betrayed him for the amusement of everyone else on the set. This was still early in our relationship; we were learning about each other. It was long before I'd built up the kind of reservoir of goodwill that allowed me to make this kind of silly mistake. Leonard stalked angrily off the set. He confronted me later, telling me he wanted nothing to do with me, that he thought I was a real son of a bitch. My apology seemed hollow. He didn't say a word to me that wasn't in the script for at least a week.

But by the time we filmed that episode, Leonard had established his character's character. In the last scene of that particular episode, after we had secured peace on that world, Kirk told Spock that he was becoming more human all the time. Spock considered that, rolling it over in his mind and testing the concept, then responded, perfectly, "Captain, there's no reason for me to stand here and be insulted!"

Spock eventually became a lasting archetype for an unemotional person. Even decades later, when *New York Times* columnist Maureen Dowd wanted to make the point that President Obama was dispassionate and distant, she referred to him as Spock. Spock's lack of emotion became a central theme of the show. In fact, a lot of the humor in the show came from the constant sparring between the very human Bones McCoy and Spock. In one episode, for example, Spock comments, "He reminds me of someone I knew in my youth."

To which the surprised Bones responds, "Why, Spock, I didn't know you had one."

In another episode, McCoy explains to Spock, "Medical men are trained in logic."

And the wry Spock feigns surprise as he suggests, "Trained? Judging from you, I would have guessed it was trial and error."

One of the most poignant moments in the original series took place at the end of the first-season episode "This Side of Paradise." After being exposed to aphrodisiacal spores, Spock is able to express his love to Leila Kalomi, a woman he had known a few years earlier on Earth. But when the effect of the spores wears off, he is left once again without the ability to feel emotions. "I am what I am, Leila," he explains to her logically. "And if there are self-made purgatories, then we all have to live in them. Mine can be no worse than someone else's."

And as she wipes away her tears, Leila asks, knowing the answer, "Do you mind if I say I still love you?"

At the conclusion of the episode, the *Enterprise* has once again restored order on the planet, and the crew is making preparations to depart that galaxy. Spock has been unusually quiet, so Kirk finally points out, "We haven't heard much from you about Omicron Ceti Three, Mr. Spock."

In response, Spock says evenly, "I have little to say about it, Captain, except that for the first time in my life I was happy."

It is difficult for people who aren't actors

to appreciate the talent it took to create a character that has become a part of American cultural history, the enigmatic Jay Gatsby of the twenty-third century, destined to be played and interpreted by other actors. In less capable hands, it could have been a very one-dimensional role, but he was able to create a dynamic inner life for his character. Of course, the real test for an actor is the way an audience relates to his or her character. Do they empathize with that character? Root for that character? Fear that character? Or do they laugh at that character and not care at all about his or her fate? It actually was surprising how many people found things in their own lives to relate to a thin, dour man with funny-looking ears, rather than the heroic captain, clearly a man of sterling virtue! While I certainly don't know, I suspect the fact that Spock didn't easily fit in with the crew was a feeling many people recognized. I remember during our first season, a young girl wrote to Spock through a fan magazine: "I know that you are half Vulcan and half human and you have suffered because of this. My mother is Negro and my father is white and I am told this makes me a half-breed. . . . The Negroes don't like me because I don't look like them, the white kids don't like me because I don't exactly look like them either. I guess I'll never have any friends."

Now, truthfully, I will never know for certain if Leonard actually wrote the response or if someone in the network's publicity department did, but as I read this, I could hear Leonard's calming voice, and knowing him as well as I did and watching his concern for other people over the many years, I strongly believe this response was his. While answering her, he filled in some of the blanks about Spock's backstory and the childhood that shaped the being. Growing up on Vulcan of mixed races, he wrote, Spock

was very lonely and no one understood him. And Spock was heartbroken because he wasn't popular. But it was only the *need* for popularity that was ruining his happiness. . . . It takes a great deal of courage to turn your back on popularity and go out on your own. . . .

Now, there's a little voice inside each of us that tells us when we're not being true to ourselves. We should listen to that voice. . . . Spock learned he could save himself from letting prejudice get him down. He could do this by really understanding himself and knowing his own value as a person. He found he was equal to anyone who might try to put him down — equal in his own unique way.

You can do this too, if you realize the difference between popularity and true greatness. . . . Spock said to himself: 'OK, I'm not a Vulcan, so the Vulcans don't want me. My blood isn't pure Earth red blood. It's green. And my ears — well, it's obvious I'm not pure human. So they won't want me either. I must do for myself and not worry about what others think of me who really don't know me.'

Spock decided he would live up to his own personal value and uniqueness. He'd do whatever made him feel best about himself. . . . He said to himself: . . . 'I will develop myself to such a point of excellence, intelligence and brilliance that I can see through any problems and deal with any crisis. I will become such a master of my own abilities and career that there will always be a place for me.' . . . And that's what he did.

# FIVE

The relationship between Kirk and Spock remained considerably warmer than that of Shatner and Nimoy, but they had better writers. Throughout that first season, Leonard and I remained respectful, polite, and professional, but I don't remember ever even having a conversation about our personal lives. It was odd; we had a tremendous amount in common, but we hadn't found a reason to explore it. It wasn't just me; this was the first time in Leonard's career that he really was a star, his name was painted on his dressing room door, and it was clear that he was enjoying success after seventeen years of being what's-his-name, that dark-and-gloomy-looking guy.

Generally, we went our own ways, meeting on the set. But whatever I was feeling, it all came to a head very early one morning. Spock's ears had become a popular story, and our makeup artist, Freddy Phillips, who had used his own money to get the second set of ears made, was receiving a lot of well-deserved attention. So when *TV Guide* wanted to do a photo story about making up Spock, Leonard agreed. But no one bothered to tell me about it.

It took as long as three hours to apply Leonard's makeup, while mine took about fifteen minutes, so he was always in makeup hours before I was. I arrived at work one morning, and as I sat in my chair, reviewing my lines, making my usual wonderfully clever remarks, getting ready for the day, I noticed a photographer snapping pictures. I had no idea who he was or how he had gotten permission to invade this actor's sanctuary. I believe I had approval of still photographs taken on the set. I wasn't especially excited about the possibility that candid shots might be published. So I asked who he was and what he was doing there. In my memory, I asked politely. There may be another side to that story. When I found out, I called the producers to complain. Soon, someone came down and asked the photographer to leave. There, situation settled.

Except it wasn't. This was an important opportunity for Leonard. After seventeen years of working in obscurity, one of the most popular magazines in America was featuring him in a story. Leonard decided he wasn't going to continue being made up until the photographer returned. When that didn't happen, he got up and confronted me in my trailer.

"Did you order the photographer out?" he asked.

"Order" seemed like a harsh word, but not an inaccurate one. "I did," I admitted. "I didn't want him there."

Years later, Leonard remembered this conversation very clearly. He told me, "It was approved by Roddenberry. It was approved by the head of the studio. It was approved by publicity."

To which he remembers me responding, "Well, it wasn't approved by me." Harsh words, and I must have been a lot more envious than I remember being at the time. But in my defense, actors can be very defensive when they believe they are protecting their careers. That's not much of a defense, but it's the best I've got. And years later, if I really remembered saying this, I certainly would have regretted it.

Leonard stood his ground, saying, "You mean to tell me that I've got to get approval from you to have my picture taken?" I do see the question mark at the end of that last sentence, but I suspect Leonard did not intend it to be a question. George Takei described Leonard's demeanor as "cold rage." He went to his dressing room, the one with his name painted on the door.

Several executives came down from wherever executives come down from and met privately with Leonard. Then this group came to my dressing room. Meanwhile, the rest of the cast, all in costume and ready to go to work, instead went to the commissary for breakfast. When they returned, the set was still dark. The executives were shuttling back and forth trying to establish a détente. The cast filled the morning doing nothing, until someone suggested that they take an early lunch. So they went back to the commissary. With the tight production schedule we were forced to maintain because of our limited budget, this constituted an expensive crisis. Roddenberry finally came down and negotiated a peace — I have no idea what it was — but we all went back to work.

Looking back on that particular event, I don't think I truly understood the source of his anger until many years later. And I should have. Just being in this profession I should have. An actor is the most dominated person in show business. Producers hire and fire based on who knows what. Writers put words in the actor's mouth. Directors tell them where to move. Critics put the responsibility for the end product entirely on the actor, whose performance may be the result of bad writers working with a poor director. So just imagine what can happen when an actor finally gets in a position of power. There are some people in this profession who take out the frustrations that have built up on other people. That wasn't Leonard. But Leonard had spent seventeen years going from job to job, like we all do, wondering: What am I going to do next? How am I going to pay the rent? How am I going to pay for my children's education? What do I do when I get older? Will I be able to age into character parts? And then Leonard found a home in *Star Trek*. He found a place to excel. Finally, he had a job that was going to get him attention, a job that inevitably would lead to other jobs. And then this guy Shatner gets in the way of all that for his own reasons.

No wonder Leonard was upset. Had I been cognizant of any of this, I would have been different; I don't know how, but I would have been much more there, I would have been understanding and supportive, but who considers all those things when they are in the middle of an unpleasant confrontation?

It did not help matters that Leonard remained aloof between takes. He certainly didn't join in the casual camaraderie usually found on a set. Generally, an actor puts on his or her character when the camera starts rolling. We're wearing the costumes, we've got the makeup on, and we ease into the voice and mannerisms for the scene. When the scene is over, we're ourselves in costume; in those days, it meant having a cigarette and a cup of coffee, a little friendly conversation, what'd you do over the weekend, how was your son's football game, and then back to work. At the end of the day, it's back to real life.

But that didn't work for Leonard. It took such an enormous emotional investment in being Spock that he didn't escape it, even when the bright lights were dimmed. There's very little downtime when making a TV show; you finish one scene and move right on to the next one. It's wham-bam for twelve hours; you have ten pages to get done that day, you're on-screen, you're offscreen. Next, c'mon, let's go, great, next. Either Leonard or I, or both of us, were pretty much in every scene. Leonard didn't have the time to put on Spock and take him off, so between scenes, he stayed very much in character, which meant keeping a distance from the rest of us who were relaxing. We all would be sitting around, and I would be entertaining my fellow actors with jokes about two actors arguing — "I'm playing nothing, so you can't" — and everyone would laugh with recognition — except Leonard. He would sit staring at me and rolling the joke over in his mind, analyzing the humor, parsing the language, digesting the deeper meaning. "I found it very difficult to turn it off and on," he told me. "So stepping out of the set, sitting in a chair waiting for the next setup, I couldn't shift out of the character."

It wasn't just during the workday, he explained, "I was in that character more hours during the week than I was in my own. I spent more time as Spock than as Nimoy, twelve hours a day five days a week. That's most of your waking life."

That was beyond my understanding. Maybe that was because our approach to the work was so different; at the end of the day, I was able to shed Kirk or T. J. Hooker or Denny Crane or any of the many other characters I became and resume my adventures as Bill Shatner.

In fact, an odd thing happened: Leonard began adapting some of Spock's characteristics into his own life. He became very comfortable with Spock's clear, precisely punctuated speech pattern, his thoughtful pauses before responding, and his broadly accepting rather than judgmental social attitudes. "I found them comforting," he said, "and by osmosis they became part of me." Decades after the show ended, he told a journalist, "My personality changed. I became more rational. I became more logical. I became more thoughtful. I became less emotional. . . . I could feel it especially on the weekends."

It probably was not a huge transition. As long as I knew Leonard, he always was somewhat restrained in behavior and emotion. He wasn't someone who had great, loud bursts of unrestrained exuberance. He was thoughtful, calm, and maybe even a little contained. I don't think anyone ever described Leonard Nimoy as boisterous. There is a photograph that his son, Adam, found while producing and directing a documentary about his father. It was a picture of Leonard with his close friend, writer Don Siegel. Siegel is whispering in Leonard's ear, and whatever he has said, Leonard's head is thrown back, and he is laughing hysterically. "It was very infrequent to see my dad cut loose like that," Adam said. "It's not even a very good photo, but it's so interesting to capture that moment because we just didn't see a lot of that from him, that kind of joy, unbridled and unchecked. He was very much like his parents, who were very reserved, who held things in check. They were very unemotive, very even-keeled, and Dad was that way as well."

Now that doesn't mean Leonard didn't have a sense of humor, but he didn't tell jokes as much as make astute humorous comments. He was fascinated by technology, although not especially knowledgeable about cutting-edge advances. He certainly did not have any of Spock's expertise, but scientists loved to show their work to him. At one point, for example, he was visiting Caltech, and several brilliant young scientists were thrilled to explain their projects to him. I suspect Leonard had some vague idea what they were talking about, but he certainly didn't understand the intricacies. Leonard liked to tell the story, "They would look at me and ask, 'What do you think?' "

Leonard nodded thoughtfully, then very quietly and very sagely replied, "You're on the right track."

He also loved being involved in pranks and practical jokes, whether he was the pranker or the prankee! Actors often play pranks on each other as a means of dealing with the boredom on a set between takes. Once, I remember, our target was Dee Kelley. Everybody loved Dee Kelley. He was a large and compassionate human being, as well as a fine actor. But one night while we were shooting, he had made the mistake of confiding in me that he was somewhat concerned that his memory was slipping. Naturally, I was supportive and compassionate; naturally. In the commissary the next morning, I enlisted Leonard's assistance. When DeForest put a bagel in the toaster, I whispered to Leonard, "Occupy Dee's attention." Leonard began singing a song from *Man of La Mancha,* and Dee turned to watch him. I unloaded the toaster, putting the bagel away. After a moment or two, DeForest walked over the toaster, the toaster popped up — and there was nothing in it.

Hmm. He thought about it a second, then sliced a second bagel and put it in the toaster. This time Leonard called over to him and asked him how he liked this song, then sang a song from *Fiddler on the Roof.* I pushed up the toaster and shoved the bagel in my mouth. A minute later, Dee came back, popped up the toaster again — and took a deep breath. He stared at the toaster, trying to reconcile the facts as he remembered them. Naturally, he didn't want to say anything to anyone, but it appeared his greatest fear was coming true. He glanced around furtively, hoping no one would notice his distress. And then his eyes settled on me, and he saw me choking on a bagel, trying desperately to keep myself from laughing — and shook his head in acknowledgment that he'd been fooled.

Arguably my greatest prank involved Mr. Nimoy. By the end of our first season, we had forged our own bonds. We had become united — mostly against the production company and the network. Leonard and I had worked out our differences, and while we hadn't yet become friends, we certainly were getting along. So it was a ripe time for me to instigate. The soundstage on which we worked was quite a distance from the studio commissary. As we only got a half-hour break for lunch, when it was time, we all raced to get there as rapidly as possible. Often, there was a long line being served lunch, a line that moved slowly, so if you were on the end of that line, there was a chance you would go hungry that day.

I had been on the track team in school. I was pretty fast, especially for an actor. Leonard was less athletic than I was, and although he had long legs, he did not move nearly as fast. Perhaps those ears caught the wind and held him back. But the result was that I got my lunch every day, and sometimes Leonard did not. But Leonard was a very resourceful man; he figured things out. One day, lunch was called, and I dashed outside and started running — and seconds later Leonard came speeding past me on a bicycle, leaving me far behind. When I got to the commissary, he was already being served — and my memory is that he looked at me triumphantly. He later described it as "the logical thing to do." But it was a victory that could not be allowed to stand.

I felt he had showed a disregard for the unspoken rules of fair play by employing mechanical means. His bike was easy to find; he had written his name on it in large letters. With the assistance of other members of the cast and crew, who also did not like to be outsmarted or outsprinted, we tied a rope to his bike and hoisted it into the rafters. Two electricians trained spotlights on it. At lunchtime, he dashed outside — to discover his bike was gone. When he complained, I suggested, "Come back inside and turn your head to the heavens. Look to the stars!" And so he looked up and saw his bike in the flies of the stage. Everybody was laughing. Well, okay, not quite everybody.

I wanted to make sure such a terrible thing like that never happened again to an esteemed member of our cast. To make certain of that, I brought a good lock and chained and secured his bicycle to a fire hydrant. When he came outside and saw it, he demanded, "Who did that?" I stood right up and shrugged. "I don't know. I was wondering that myself."

The next day he came to work with bolt cutters. Now, I am a lover of animals; I ride horses and love dogs, especially Dobermans. Wonderful dogs, big, wonderful dogs. In fact, on occasion, I would bring one of my Dobermans with me to the studio, and keep the dog in my dressing room. So when I came outside later that day and saw Leonard's bike there unattended, I worried that someone might take it, so to help my friend Leonard, I put it in my dressing room for security purposes only. When they called lunch and Leonard went outside and discovered his bike was missing, once again he demanded to know what had happened to it. I pressed my palm earnestly to my chest and told him about my fears and directed him to my dressing room. "Door's open," I suspect I told him. I may have added that the best way to stop a Doberman in midair is to reach in and grab its tongue. Then I went to lunch.

Leonard claimed later that he had employed the Vulcan nerve pinch, but it didn't work. "Those dogs are meaner than you," were his actual words, "and that's not easy." I gave him back his bicycle, believing my point had been made. Apparently, it hadn't. The next day Leonard drove his car, a large Buick, onto the lot, parked it directly outside the soundstage, put his bicycle in the backseat, and locked the car.

I did not personally tow that car away. But I did feel it might be a hazard, so I arranged for it to be done. I believe that was when Leonard finally agreed that he would be running to the commissary.

Whatever attributes the audience attributed to Spock, and probably Leonard, the character resonated with them. Kids began wearing Spock ears, and Leonard received piles and piles of fan mail, far more than any of the other cast members. When he was out in public, people would greet him with a raised hand or wish him, "Live long and prosper." Ironically, many of them came from women who, according to pop psychologists, were attracted by his alienation. On a different level, I experienced the same thing. People began addressing me as

"Captain" or "Kirk." That was a new experience for me. I'd had professional success, I'd played a role in some major movies, people recognized me, but I had never before been called by my character's name. It was odd, and in some ways, it made me uncomfortable. I'm not quite sure why, but it did. I wondered, *What is that all about? It's crazy.* So often I didn't acknowledge it, or I disparaged it.

If I was feeling that confusion, that ambivalence, I can't imagine what Leonard must have been going through. Other actors had become famous because of the characters they played. Jim Arness was *Gunsmoke*'s Marshall Matt Dillon. Robert Stack gained recognition as Eliot Ness on *The Untouchables.* Edd Brynes was a teen idol as Kookie in *77 Sunset Strip.* But none of those characters achieved the historic popularity of Spock. Fans of those shows were thrilled to meet Jim Arness, Robert Stack, or Edd Byrnes — but our fans wanted to meet Mr. Spock.

Perhaps the strangest thing was that eventually Leonard became somewhat ambivalent about his relationship with Spock. Spock made Leonard's career. In each of the three years the show was on the air, Leonard was nominated for an Emmy as best supporting actor. *TV Guide* named Spock one of the fifty greatest characters in TV history. Leonard became well known and in demand because of the original series. But the new fear, replacing "I will never work again," was that he was so strongly identified as Spock that he could never escape him. For someone who proudly described himself as a character actor, being so strongly typecast he could not play other roles was a terrifying possibility. His first autobiography, published in 1975, was titled *I Am Not Spock.* The title, he explained, came from a meeting in an airport, in which a woman introduced him to her daughter as Spock — although the child was never convinced. It also came from the publisher's desire to profit from the popularity of Spock as well as create a little controversy. It was not, Leonard always insisted, meant to be a statement about his feelings about Spock, and he said if he ever had the opportunity to portray any fictional character, without hesitation he would choose Spock. And several years later, when he did write a second autobiography, it was titled *I Am Spock.*

He had come full circle.

While *Star Trek* initially became incredibly popular among a core audience, it didn't achieve the kind of success the network had envisioned. Leonard always believed they didn't really understand the show. They expected an action show with monsters, futuristic weapons, and great battles in space; that wasn't the show Roddenberry wanted to produce. So we never got the full promotional push from the network. Scheduling always was a problem. They moved us around, making it almost impossible for us to build an audience. We would come to work each week secretly harboring the fear that we had been canceled. The first season the show was broadcast at 7:30 Thursday nights, which was early enough for us to attract our target, high school and college kids, young professionals, and young married couples. The second season we were on a little later, and our audience got smaller. Our third year, we originally were moved to Monday nights at 7:30, the perfect spot for us. But doing that required moving the top-rated live comedy show *Laugh-In* back a half hour; when that show's producer, George Schlatter, objected, NBC moved *Star Trek* to Friday 10:00 P.M. That was the worst possible time slot for us; our young audience wasn't home watching television on a Friday night. And those people who were home were in a different universe.

The show just never had the support of the network. We worked on an extremely tight budget, which meant we had a difficult six-day shooting schedule — and for the third season, they even reduced that budget by $15,000 an episode. If we went over budget, we weren't permitted to beam down to another planet in the next episode; instead we did what was referred to as a "bottle episode" — the entire episode had to be shot on the existing *Enterprise* sets. To ensure there was no overtime, we ended every day at precisely 6:18. Even if we were in the middle of a scene, we stopped at 6:18 so the crew could clean up, put everything away, and be done by 6:30. The CBS show *Mission: Impossible* was filming on the adjoining soundstages and had an eight- or sometimes nine-day schedule — and then an extra day to shoot inserts, the clever little devices they used to stop the weekly revolution in an unnamed Eastern European country. They needed that time — that was a visual show — whereas of necessity, we were a verbal show. *Star Trek* depended on the interplay between the cast; *MI* depended more on what the camera showed the audience. It was amazing how much we accomplished with so little money. Our special effects truly were minimal. Our doors, which seemed to open magically, were manually operated. All the sound effects, essentially whooshing when the doors were operated and occasional death rays, were added in postproduction. For a show supposedly taking place three centuries in the future, we relied on rudimentary, inexpensive technology.

What made the show work, in addition to the relationships between the members of the crew, were the stories we told each week. *Star Trek* was a tribute to the great tradition of science fiction, in which future civilizations were used to tell contemporary morality tales, tales about subjects that couldn't be addressed for various reasons at the time. Leonard was a serious man; he always cared about the issues that affected people's lives. I like to believe I've lived my life the same way. While both of us had found ways to do meaningful work, Leonard in plays like *Deathwatch* and Yiddish theater, me in great movies like *Judgment at Nuremburg,* we also had done a lot of shoot-'em-ups and cop stories — the cotton candy of the entertainment industry. So when we got our scripts each week, we always were interested in seeing which controversial topics our writers were attacking that week and how they had cleverly managed to get away with it. "That's what made *Star Trek* meaningful for me," Leonard explained to journalist Paul Fischer in 2009. "We tackled some very interesting issues through the years: racial issues, economic issues, ecological issues. Writers were given an opportunity in *Star Trek* to tell stories about issues that they could not tackle in other television shows." On different episodes, we explored grand issues like authoritarianism, class warfare, imperialism, human and alien rights, and, always, the insanity of war. Maybe the most controversial thing we did get away with was the first interracial kiss ever shown on American television. It actually caused that particular episode to be banned on several Southern affiliate stations. Leonard and I, DeForest Kelley, George Takei, Walker Koenig, Jimmy Doohan, Majel Barrett, and Nichelle Nichols were doing work we were proud of doing. And every once in a while, we'd get confirmation what we were doing was important.

After the first season, both Leonard and Nichelle Nichols began getting the types of offers they'd been working for their entire careers. Nichelle had been brought up in the musical theater, and her dream was to appear on Broadway. She told Roddenberry she had decided to leave the show and move to New York. He asked her to think about it for a few days and, coincidently, the following night she went to an NAACP fundraiser in Beverly Hills. During the party, one of the hosts asked her to meet a man who described himself as her greatest fan. *Another Trekkie,* she thought, one of the growing legion of fans of the show. And then she turned around to greet Dr. Martin Luther King Jr. "I am your greatest fan," he told her. "I'm that Trekkie." Nichelle told him how much she regretted not being out there marching with him. "No, no, no," he said. "No, you don't understand. We don't need you to march. You are marching. You are reflecting what we are fighting for."

Nichelle told him how incredibly flattered she was, then admitted that she was leaving the show, that she'd told Gene Roddenberry the day before. He shook his head and said, "You cannot do that. Don't you understand what this man has achieved? For the first time, we are being seen the world over as we should be seen. This is the only show that my wife, Coretta, and I will allow our little children to stay up and watch."

Apparently, Whoopi Goldberg told Nichelle a similar story, remembering turning on the show when she was nine years old and seeing Nichelle, which caused her to run through her apartment screaming, "Come quick! Come quick! There's a black lady on TV, and she ain't no maid!"

While perhaps not exactly typical, it was the kind of reaction we were getting. Roddenberry's objective had been achieved — and no character was more important to that than Leonard's Mr. Spock. It was those loyal fans, and Gene Roddenberry, that kept us on the air for three seasons. While we were still shooting second-season episodes, we began hearing rumors that NBC was planning to cancel the show. In response, Roddenberry very quietly orchestrated a massive letter-writing campaign through fan clubs. "If thousands of fans just sit around moaning about the death of *Star Trek*," Bjo Trimble, a friend of Roddenberry, wrote, "they will get exactly what they deserve: *Gomer Pyle!*" The threat worked. Either because those people loved our show or were terrified of *Gomer Pyle,* the network received more than one million letters pleading with the executives not to cancel the show. It probably was the greatest display of fan loyalty in television history, and NBC respected that loyalty and canceled the planned cancelation. That marked the beginning of the most unusual relationship between a show and its audience in television history and perhaps in all the annals of entertainment.

# Six

It might well have been the British beer ad that marked the beginning of our friendship. When we did the original series, none of the actors were well paid. Apparently, Leonard was paid $1,250 an episode our first season, more than everyone else but less than I. We didn't even get paid residuals; it's possible that no show has been run more often in syndication than the original series, yet none of us have ever received a penny from that. The network and Paramount also retained all merchandising rights. That was a keen source of resentment by everybody in the cast, but notably Leonard. Spock was hot! Spock was marketable, and the network sold him. His likeness began popping up all over the place, and Leonard grew progressively angrier. Mr. Spock was the result of seventeen years of him struggling to learn and survive and get better as an actor. But what might finally have set Leonard off was discovering during a visit to London that Spock's image had been plastered on billboards selling Heineken. Leonard was justifiably furious that the studio was using his face to sell beer in Britain — especially because he didn't know about it or receive any income from it.

Unfortunately, Leonard had become used to that type of treatment. Several months into our first season, an agent offered him $2,000 to make a personal appearance in Boston on a Saturday afternoon. Even after the agent took his 10 percent fee, Leonard would make more money in a few hours than he made in a week doing the show. This was a huge offer for him; it was the first time he'd ever had this type of opportunity. His only problem was that in order to be there on time, he had to get a 6:00 P.M. flight Friday night, which meant leaving the set a bit more than an hour early. It wasn't really an issue; with enough notice, we easily could film around him. He asked Roddenberry for permission to make the flight. What happened then was something Leonard never forgot.

"I didn't get an answer from the producers for a few days, and the agent wanted me to make the commitment," Leonard explained. "Finally, I was told Gene Roddenberry wanted to see me. I went to his office, and we spoke for a few minutes. Then he said, 'I understand you want to get out early Friday.' " That was true, Leonard said, then told Roddenberry about the $2,000 offer.

As he told me this story, he shook his head in disbelief. He was truly stunned when Roddenberry replied, "I've just started a company called Lincoln Enterprises. We're going to do some merchandising of *Star Trek* memorabilia, but we also want to represent actors for personal appearances. I'd like to represent you for this appearance. The fee is twenty percent." Leonard told Roddenberry that he already was paying an agent 10 percent and didn't understand why he should be forced to pay him too. Roddenberry looked at him and said coldly, "The difference between your agent and me is that your agent can't get you out of here at five o'clock on Friday, and I can. And all it'll cost you is twenty percent."

Leonard's response was consistent with the way he led his life. "I can't do that to this agent," he said. "He got me the job."

Roddenberry's reply accurately described the thought process of the suits about actors. "I will never forget his exact words," Leonard said. " 'Well, you're just going to have to bow down and say *master.*' "

"You got the wrong guy," Leonard snapped, then walked angrily out of his office. In that instance Roddenberry relented, and Leonard made his flight. "But while we worked together for years afterward, that was the end of any semblance of friendship between Gene Roddenberry and myself."

As the popularity of Spock continued to rise, Leonard's relationship with the producers continued to get worse. It got so nasty that the producers sent him a memo informing him that he was not allowed to use the studio's pens and pencils.

The result was predictable. Until this time in his career, Leonard had been powerless; like most actors, he was always a whim away from being fired or not getting the job. Now that he finally had actual power, those seventeen years of slights, seventeen years of being easily dismissed as a working character actor, it gave him the backbone to stand up for not only his rights but the rights of every member of the cast. Several years later, Filmation obtained the rights to produce an animated version of the show. They hired Leonard and me, and they hired Jimmy Doohan to play Scotty and do all the other male voices and Majel Barrett as Nurse Chapel and the other female voices. Their explanation for not hiring the other actors was that they were working on a limited budget and couldn't afford them. When Leonard learned about that, he said he wouldn't do the show. "This isn't *Star Trek,*" he told them. "*Star Trek* is about diversity, and the two people who most represent that are George Takei and Nichelle Nichols, and if they're not going to be part of it, then I'm not interested." The company had no choice; without Leonard or me, there was no *Star Trek.* This was long before the *Star Trek* franchise was generating small mountains of revenue, so the salary offered to Leonard made a difference. He had learned how to use his power. They hired those actors.

At the same time, I was having my own problems with Gene Roddenberry. He had created a quasi-military medal that Lincoln Enterprises was marketing. To promote sales of this award, he wanted to use it on the show; I was supposed to pin it on a crew member. This awards ceremony had absolutely nothing to do with the plot, and I refused to get involved. They prevailed upon Leonard and somehow convinced him to do it.

Both Leonard and I had a complicated relationship with Gene Roddenberry. He had many talents, but often tact wasn't among them. While he had the vision to create this amazing world, he also could waste time focusing on petty ways to generate insignificant dollars. And he was not easily swayed; when he believed in something, he didn't easily relent, whether he was dealing with actors or the network. It was Gene who convinced Leonard to put on those ears, and it was also Gene who mounted the fan-based letter-writing campaign that kept us on the air. Leonard once described his relationship with Roddenberry "like a father-son relationship; sometimes it was great, and sometimes it was really bad." Obviously that was the reason Leonard at times was so bitterly disappointed by Gene's actions. I never felt that way. Gene certainly could be paternalistic, but I don't think I had a need for approval at that point in my career. Whatever the sometimes difficult dynamics of their relationship, without question, Roddenberry and Leonard both lived long and prospered because of it. They needed each other — we all needed each other — and looking back, it is far more important to focus on Gene's creative genius than the family fights we endured.

After we'd shot our first thirteen episodes, writer/producer Gene Coon became the producer while Roddenberry was elevated to executive producer. His main function seemed to be figuring out how to squeeze every penny out of this show before it ran dry. He sold everything imaginable. Cinematographers shoot what is known as a light strip before each scene to check the lighting. It's usually ten or so frames, only enough frames to make sure the set is properly lit. These frames usually get thrown away. Roddenberry sold each one of them.

Most shows produce some kind of gag reel; it's just a few minutes of actual bloopers combined with jokes we set up. It is made for the entertainment of the cast and crew. There often are a lot of inside jokes. We did one, for example, that began with Spock shooting an arrow — followed by a scene is which Kirk is being rushed into a cave with an arrow sticking high out of his crotch. It was a joke with many levels of meaning, and it was not intended for the public to see it. Roddenberry spliced together highlights from these reels and sold them. I first heard about it when someone told me a friend of his had seen it in a bar.

It took some time, but Leonard and I began to understand that we had far more power working together than working individually. Perhaps coincidentally, perhaps not, but at just about the same time as Kirk and Spock were gaining popularity, two of the greatest pitchers in baseball, future Hall of Famers Sandy Koufax and Don Drysdale, had changed tradition by negotiating their annual contracts with the Dodgers together. The story was in the headlines of the papers for several weeks. Their holdout forced the Dodgers to give each of them a larger raise than they would have received individually. I don't remember if that originally influenced Leonard and me or not, but we made the decision to negotiate together. We didn't make any kind of agreement beyond the fact that we'd talk to each other whenever there was a problem or an opportunity. At times, we brought that power to bear on script changes, on contractual clauses, and certainly where money was concerned. And later, as *Star Trek* grew into a multibillion-dollar franchise, our power to affect that was enormous. We also were offered many other commercial opportunities to exploit our roles, in addition to appearances at the conventions, which forced us into a continuing relationship. It took a couple of years, but the more time we spent together, the more we began to discover how much we liked being with each other. Unlike any other show or movie on which I've worked, where the end of the shoot invariably marked the end of many friendships, the end of the series after three seasons was just the beginning of a friendship that was to last a lifetime.

Leonard was not an easy person to get close to; he seemed comfortable keeping a respectful distance between himself and the rest of the cast. As I later learned, it was a lot more than sustaining the alienation of Spock that kept him apart from the rest of the cast. While we were filming the show, Leonard was keeping a secret; at that time, he was a functioning alcoholic.

I only knew about this later, when Leonard was comfortable enough to talk about it publicly. Like so many other things in his life, this was an important lesson he had learned, and he wanted to share it. He wanted to save people the pain that he had endured. Unfortunately for me, when I needed to listen to him most, I refused to accept his advice.

He had started drinking regularly sometime during our second or third season, he told me on film while we were filming our documentary, *Mind Meld.* "Until then," he said, "no problem. I'd have a glass of wine or a drink after work, maybe two, it was no problem. But the ritual became so important to me, so ingrained, because I looked forward to that release at the end of the pressure of the day.

"My secretary was in the habit of bringing me a drink in a paper cup. The minute we finished the last shot, I would drink. And then it became a series of drinks. Little by little, before I knew it, I was drinking more and more because my addictive personality was taking over. As many alcoholics can do, I hid it at work. I never allowed it to affect my work. As long as I never drank while I was working, I had this illusion of control. I lied to myself a lot: I don't work drunk; I don't drink at all in connection to my work. I can wait."

I never saw it. I never saw Leonard drunk. I never saw him miss a moment of work or be less than completely professional. The fact is that I had no understanding of alcoholism. I thought everybody was like me — when there was something I needed to do, I did it. Leonard and I both smoked heavily when we were making the original series, for example. I smoked so much that when I kissed any of my three little girls, they would scrunch up their faces and tell me, "Daddy, you smell." I didn't like my kids turning away from me because I reeked of smoke, so I became determined to give it up.

It wasn't easy. I quit cold turkey; I just put down the pack of cigarettes and never picked it up again. I went through some tough times fighting it. Leonard liked to remind me of the day I walked off the set as we finished shooting a scene and kept walking through the soundstage and out the door, finally stopping and shouting in desperation, "I want a cigarette!" Somehow I managed to break that habit. Leonard smoked too, and he knew I was fighting my demon as he was fighting his. The difference between us was something psychologists understand; I do not have an addictive personality. It's possible Leonard did. For a long time, I believed it was a matter of will; if you wanted to do it, you could. I was wrong, terribly, terribly wrong.

Leonard tried to stop both smoking and drinking at about the same time, an almost impossible task. "I thought maybe I could smoke a little bit," he told me when we discussed this. "But I can't do that. If I smoked a little, I ended up smoking a lot. If I drank a little, I ended up drinking a lot. And within a matter of a year or two, I developed a major problem with alcohol. It reached the point where I could no longer control how much I was drinking.

"I would make myself promises I couldn't

keep. That's how I started losing my self-respect. I'd be drinking midday on a Saturday or Sunday and then passing out. I'd go to bed at four o'clock in the afternoon and sleep through the next day, missing a party in my own home. People would come in, and I'd be out. I would promise myself, this weekend that's not going to happen. This weekend I'm not going to have more than a beer or two on Saturday and not before two o'clock. By 11:00, I'd have a beer, by 3:00 or 4:00, I'd pass out again. Eventually, I realized I had become an alcoholic."

There is no single, logical explanation for why some people become alcoholics. I'm sure there are complex emotional and physical reasons. I've had to deal with it in my own life; against Leonard's advice, I married an alcoholic. Although both Leonard and I tried desperately to help her, we could never reach the source of her pain. The situation never got better, and she died in a terrible accident, drowning in our pool after drinking heavily. So yes, I do know about alcoholics; I know how they become experts at fooling the people around them, I know the pain they inflict on other people, and I know that they can't help it. Who knows why Leonard began drinking? We never got to the why.

But I suspect one contributing factor was that the reality of success disappointed him greatly. As he said, "I had this fantasy that with *Star Trek* I had found a home as an actor. Suddenly I had a parking space with a permanent sign, a dressing room with my name painted on it that was going to be there for a few months at least. That was extraordinary for me. I thought I'd found a family. The writers and producers were the father figures, and the actors and actresses were my brothers and sisters. I looked forward to coming to work with my creative, artistic family every day. And then I began to discover that the studio was not necessarily my friend, or my parent, that they were contract people.

"Rather than supporting me, they were asking, 'How much are we paying him? If he asks for more, tell him we'll get somebody else to wear the ears. He wants a phone in his dressing room? Is it in his contract? No phone, no. He wants to get off on Friday — no, he has to work until 6:15.' There was no give, no viewing in a familial way. It made me very confused and very angry. It caused me to go into therapy."

In most professions, people get to release much of the tension from their jobs when they get home. Filming a TV series is so all life-consuming that after-hours outlets often don't exist. In fact, sometimes the tensions caused by the work serve to magnify existing problems at home. There is no place to turn for relief. When you're filming, there is no time for anything else, including your family. My family life suffered tremendously when we were making *Star Trek,* and it certainly contributed to my divorce. For Leonard, the series seemed like a life preserver. "I'd caught a wave, and I didn't know how long it would last," he told me. "I was obsessed by getting the most out of it I possibly could. Any opportunity I had to grab, I had to suck away protection money, security for the future in case I had to go back to what I was before." The result was that his marriage suffered, and his relationship with his children was strained. As he once described it, "I minored in family and majored in career."

As his son, Adam, explained it, "He was so involved with his career that he was not connected to family issues. At the beginning, we loved Spock. When I watched him on stage before they even aired the show, looking at photographs he brought home of himself in his wardrobe, the whole family was into it. At the beginning, we loved the whole ride. But then things changed. It was difficult to get his attention. There was a lot of conflict. Eventually, I started to think, you know, enough of Spock. I mean, we've seen enough of Spock. Everybody loves Spock, but I wish Spock was more of a family guy."

Leonard's wife, Sandi, was a force of her own. She was a participant in life, an activist in the cultural shifts of the 1960s. She apparently decorated their home in the big and bright images of the counterculture movement, wore the groovy clothes, and loved rock and roll. She and Leonard both participated in the movements of the time; they were involved in the antiwar demonstrations, strongly supported peace candidates like Eugene McCarthy and George McGovern and even participated in "love-ins," where young people expressed — sometimes *really* expressed — their sexual freedom. About that, he once recalled, "It wasn't quite group sex — but there was a lot of embracing."

Leonard's commitment to work inevitably forced Sandi to become more and more independent. Like so many working actors, he missed a lot of his children's childhoods; Sandi became their role model, providing the unconditional parental love that they could not get from their father. I suspect that tore Leonard apart; he was finally able to provide some security for his family, but the cost was that he could not be with them.

How much this contributed to his drinking I have no idea. But I am certain it didn't help. The surprising thing to me is that at the time, I had no idea that this nice man, who put on the ears and went to work prepared every day, was fighting these monsters. We had not yet become close friends. I don't remember ever going to his house. And he was able to control his drinking enough that it never interfered with his work. Spock didn't drink, ever. Leonard was proud of that. Even on his worst days, Leonard took pride in his professionalism.

Of course later, when it impacted my own life and he was there to help me, I began to understand the extraordinary lengths alcoholics go to in an effort to disguise their behavior.

When the show ended, the entire cast made all the usual promises of long-lasting friendship, but with a few exceptions, we saw little of each other. This was during the time that our seventy-nine regular episodes went into syndication and over several years found a much larger audience. The syndication market was just beginning to become an important revenue source for television producers, and to recoup its investment, Paramount happily sold *Star Trek* inexpensively to any local station that would buy it. The local stations ran it and reran it then ran it again, often during the day and early evening when young people were home. The ratings for what had been perceived to be a mildly successful show at best were surprisingly strong, causing other local stations to buy the show. It was the most popular hour-long show in syndication for many, many years. The audience continued to grow. I had little hints of this, as more people recognized me after the show had gone off the network than while it was running. *That's odd,* I thought at the time. But a new and incredibly loyal audience had found the *Enterprise.* Then in March 1969, a large group of *Star Trek* fans gathered in the public library in Newark, New Jersey, to show slides, listen to lectures, participate in panel discussions, and sing songs inspired by the show. This first, unofficial convention of Trekkies led to others. Trekkies? What an odd term. There were no Gunsmokers, Bonanzites, or Flintstoners — what in this world was a Trekkie? The first official convention was held in January 1972 at the Statler-Hilton in New York. These conventions brought members of the cast together regularly and marked the real beginning of my friendship with Leonard Nimoy.

After the show ended, our careers had gone in different directions. I continued making guest appearances on many of the popular series and made several TV movies, while Leonard simply moved to the next soundstage and joined the *Mission: Impossible* cast as the character Paris, a master of disguise, while touring the country starring in the one-man show he had written, *Vincent*. But throughout it all, Leonard had continued drinking — and hiding it successfully. As he admitted during an interview, "When I was performing in a play my first drink would be when the curtain came down. But that drink had to be there. When I walked into my dressing room I wanted an ice-cold gin on the rocks waiting for me. When I directed the movie *Star Trek III* my secretary knew that as soon as I said, 'Cut. That's a wrap,' I wanted a drink. And then I would drink constantly. Once I had that first drink I would not stop drinking until I passed out or fell asleep."

The fact that Leonard was continually able to function at an extremely high professional level, as well as bring his creative visions to fruition, is remarkable. I can only wonder how much more he might have accomplished if he had been sober through those years. Perhaps because there was no Internet, he also was able to keep it completely out of the media. Most of our fans would have been shocked to know that the restrained, occasionally acerbic, often wry beloved creator of Spock could be an unhappy, angry man. As he admitted, "When I was in need of a drink and it wasn't there I could get very upset. I did a lot of college lectures, many of them in small towns. When I checked into the hotel in the afternoon one of the first things I asked was how late their bar was open. That way I knew what time I had to finish and get back there. Every once in a while I'd come back to the hotel and the bar would be locked. I wanted my drink. I'd go to the front desk and say, 'You told me the bar would be open until ten o'clock. Open the *fucking* bar!' When going out I would choose restaurants that I knew had a full bar. I loved going to the theater in London because they allowed you to drink before the show and during intermission."

Leonard continued drinking as the phenomenon of *Star Trek* evolved into other television series and feature films, and Spock and Kirk became iconic American characters. "It went on for many years,"

Leonard admitted. "And the entire time I believed I was in control. But eventually I started waking up in the morning thinking, why do I want to live today? And that's when I first became concerned."

He and Sandi finally divorced in 1986. It was neither easy nor amicable. Her anger and perhaps her bitterness were evident when she told a reporter, "He left me after thirty-three years of marriage. I didn't marry a star. I married a struggling young actor right out of college. I spent the first fifteen years being the only one who believed in him and struggling with him. I believe I had a lot to do with where he is now." Even at those worst moments in his personal life, his career intruded; during one hearing, the judge actually brought a photograph of himself with Leonard into the courtroom and asked for an autograph.

Whatever the reasons for the divorce, the guilt Leonard was carrying must have been enormous. It was extremely difficult for him to tell his elderly parents about it, as they came from a time and a place in which divorce was shameful. Good people did not get divorced. We were in preparation for a movie when he finally decided it was time to leave. One morning he packed some clothes, put them in his car, and drove away from that part of his life.

Leonard was getting up the courage to tell his parents when he was informed his photograph was going to be on the cover of *Newsweek* that week. He remembered thinking, "Maybe I can bring that magazine with me, so I can tell my parents that my marriage is over, but soften the blow by showing them the magazine. Look, isn't this nice, my picture's on the cover of this important magazine." He started driving around the city, stopping at magazine stands and stores, trying to find a copy of *Newsweek*. He was told over and over that it would arrive later that afternoon. He decided he couldn't wait; if his divorce became public before he'd told his parents, they would have been mortified.

He arrived at their apartment empty-handed. He screwed up all his courage and announced, "I've left my home."

His mother smiled. "Oh? You're selling the house?"

He shook his head. "I've left Sandi. I've taken some clothes and moved out."

His father finally decided, somehow, "This is all my fault."

His mother said sadly, "Oh. Oh."

It was a terrible blow to them, an admission of great failure. There was nothing

Leonard could do to lessen their pain. But he had no choice. I know that feeling so well. He accepted the reality that he couldn't live his life for them; he had to live it for himself. Of course, the alcohol probably made it easier.

Not long afterward, he met an extraordinary woman named Susan Bay, whose cousin Michael Bay was the director of huge films. Susan was also divorced; she had previously been married to the actor John Schuck. From the very beginning, they seemed perfect for each other and would come to refer to themselves as each other's "natural husband" and "natural wife." Another cousin of Susan's, Rabbi John Rosove, once said, "She brought him out of darkness. They just opened each other's hearts and were really there for each other."

They were married in 1989. Obviously, Susan was aware of Leonard's alcoholism. "I was still drinking," Leonard admitted, "but I was deliriously happy with her. And one day I was talking to her about how different my life was with her and how happy I felt, and she asked me, 'Then why do you drink so much?'

"And I thought, *You know, she's right. I don't have to do this anymore.* So she called a friend and within hours, on a Sunday night, someone was there from Alcoholics Anonymous. He said to me, 'You can't drink a little.' We talked for two hours, and the next night I went to my first AA meeting, which was a thrill. I haven't had a drink since we had that conversation that night."

# SEVEN

None of us had been surprised when the original series ended. With our decreased budget, we had struggled through the third season feeling the quality of the show had diminished. I don't even remember our last day of filming. It certainly wasn't overly dramatic, and none of us expected to be back together as a cast ever again. The biggest concern for all of us was, this job is over, what do we do next?

When Leonard took off the ears for what he believed to be the final time, he had no real plans. He lay around his house for several months, catching up on the sleep he'd missed having to be in makeup by 6:30 A.M. The show had given him recognition and star power; in each of our three seasons, he had been nominated for an Emmy as best supporting actor. But at that time, before great movies like *Star Wars*, *Close Encounters*, and even our *Wrath of Khan*, science fiction was considered an escapist subgenre. The accolades and awards went to contemporary social dramas that made people feel good about voting for them. Leonard was flattered to be nominated by his fellow actors; in fact, when he was notified about his first nomination, he sat down and cried. Literally. After all his hard work, the acting community had recognized him.

Money was a different thing, though; the show hadn't provided long-term financial security or a continuing revenue stream. He had agreed to star in a touring stock company production of the play *A Thousand Clowns* and was in discussions to direct several TV shows when he was offered the opportunity to replace Martin Landau in the hit show *Mission: Impossible*. There had been some stories in the media that Marty and Leonard were competing, but that was never true. Leonard would never have taken a job away from another actor; he just didn't work that way. Only after it was clear that Landau was leaving the show did Leonard accept that continuing role.

Our fears of being typecast initially turned out to be unfounded. I was offered lots of different roles and worked regularly. But while we were both working hard, fans of the show would not let go so easily. Obviously, none of us saw what was coming. In fact, Leonard tried to dissuade people from wasting their time, telling a reporter, "It's tough to live with the fact that the show is off the air, but we have to face it. The crew is disbanded now. Someone was quoted as to the possibility of us all making a *Star Trek* movie, but I think such talk is bad. All it does is rekindle emotional campaigns to get the show back on the air. Every time I hear or read about such things, I try to discourage the people involved. The show is not going back on."

So Leonard was playing Paris, a master of disguise; I was appearing in TV movies like *The Andersonville Trial* or playing John Adams in John Wayne's tribute to America, *Swing Out, Sweet Land* or showing up in series like *The FBI* or *The Name of the Game* — and the Trekkies just wouldn't let go. There is no obvious explanation for the extraordinary and lasting appeal of *Star Trek.* A lot of people have suggested a lot of different reasons, and in different ways they probably are all correct. I always believed that at the core of it there was one common denominator: it was a lot of fun. But the concept and the execution created an American mythology — and a sizeable number of people couldn't get enough of it.

*Star Trek* conventions, which grew to become a multimillion-dollar business, grew out of the small science-fiction conventions dating back to the 1930s and had become popular again, maybe in response to the brutality and insanity of the Vietnam War in the late 1960s and early 1970s. These conventions were held almost entirely to celebrate the great science-fiction literature, and writers and the organizers looked down on *Star Trek* because it was a television show and not a book. They didn't even consider it real science fiction. Essentially, they pushed the Trekkies out of those conventions, forcing them to organize their own gatherings.

As I wrote in my autobiography, *Up Till Now,*

> *Star Trek* became a language that bound together a large group of people with common interests. It became a sun with great gravitational pull that drew all kinds of people to it, where they could meet others just like themselves.
>
> Wearing costumes.

Among the best-known people who attended the first official *Star Trek* Convention in New York in 1972 were Gene Roddenberry, Majel Barrett, Isaac Asimov, and Hal Clement. NASA provided an eighteen-wheeler with displays to excite visitors about our space program. There was an art show, a dealer's room, and a costume competition. The organizers expected the usual five hundred or so people who generally attended science-fiction conventions; instead, more than a thousand fans showed up. Many vendors sold out their memorabilia within hours. Within three years, twenty-three conventions were being held around the country. Thirty thousand Trekkies showed up at a convention in Chicago. Soon there was a convention being held somewhere in this country — and stretching to Europe — every weekend.

When all this started, I really wanted little to do with it. *Star Trek* was my past, and I did not want it being confused with my future. And, on some level, this whole thing made me a little uncomfortable. There was a sort of cultlike element to it. On some level, the passion of these people for a TV show scared me. Once, during our third season, as I left NBC Studios in Rockefeller Center after doing publicity, fans sort of descended on me and literally tried to rip my jacket off my back.

I turned down the first few invitations

because I thought it wasn't dignified. Actors don't go to conventions. That's for mobs! Actors act! Leonard felt differently; he didn't take the whole thing quite so seriously. Even before the conventions began, he was making personal appearances at state fairs around the country. He often would bring his guitar with him, sing a few songs, tell a few *Star Trek* stories, sign a lot of autographs. Adam Nimoy once compared it to a traveling medicine man show. Leonard was always wonderful with fans. He was patient and friendly. He attended the second convention in New York in 1973 only because he happened to be in the city at the time. He wasn't paid, and his appearance wasn't announced beforehand in case something more important came up and he had to leave. Essentially, he just showed up.

By the time I attended my first convention in 1975, organizers were paying a reasonable fee. Actually a very nice fee. I didn't know what was expected of me; one of the organizers told me, "Just be prepared for endless love and people telling you how much they love your work." *Well, it couldn't possibly be that easy,* I thought. When I walked out on stage, I had no prepared remarks; I was just going to wing it. I received a huge ovation when my name was announced, causing me to wonder what I'd done to deserve it. I'd anticipated a nice small gathering; instead, the entire room was crammed, and several thousand fans were looking at me with love. And then I realized these people had expectations I was not ready to meet. I didn't even know what they wanted from me. So I fumbled through a few remarks and then, mostly in desperation, I asked if anyone had any questions.

Eight thousand hands went up. Hallelujah! I was saved. *Oh my goodness,* I thought, *this is great.* That day I heard for the first time many of the same questions I would be asked over and over through the next few decades. What surprised me was how specific these questions were and how much knowledge these people had about the show. They actually had far more knowledge about it than I did. Truthfully, there are many, many episodes of *Star Trek* that I have never seen. I have great difficulty watching myself on screen and try to avoid it. (Yes, I know the obvious joke that might fit here; no, I'm not going to write it!) I haven't seen too much of Denny Crane or any of the many others characters I played either. I did, however, watch the movie I had made in the universal language of Esperanto, Incubus. I'd made it just before we started filming *Star Trek,* and by the time it was released, I had already forgotten how to speak the language, so like the few people who actually saw this film, I didn't understand it either.

Eventually, the convention circuit became an important revenue source for many of the cast and crew. Jimmy Doohan bought a large mobile home and drove around the country appearing at conventions. With his appearance fee and the money he earned signing autographs, he probably earned more money than he would have from acting. For several members of the crew, these conventions were practically lifesaving because they had become typecast, making it difficult for them to get meaningful work. Jimmy would walk into a casting office, for example, and be told, "We don't need a Scotsman." He probably pointed out that they didn't have one: "I'm a Canadian, and I'm Irish!"

Actors, producers, writers, anyone who had been part of it was welcome. If you hammered three nails into the set, you were a welcome guest. Leonard and I probably attended at least one hundred different conventions together, and this became the glue that cemented our friendship. At many of them, we appeared on stage together and told stories. For me, that was the most fun. Leonard loved poking fun at me for something I'd done, and the audience loved hearing about it. If I close my eyes, I can visualize Leonard pointing at me and saying in the most accusatory voice, "This is the man who stole my bicycle. He is not a nice man. What kind of man steals an alien's bicycle?"

At the beginning, I suspect, Leonard was as dubious as I was about this phenomenon. I know I wondered what type of people would spend their time dressing in costume and paying tribute to a moderately successful TV series. It's fair to say that conventional people did not attend these conventions. But I think we both came to understand how much fun these conventions were for Trekkies. These were people, for the most part, who were able to overcome their inhibitions and put on a pair of alien ears; they didn't waste time worrying what other people thought. They were simply having fun. Later in his life, Leonard was asked what words of wisdom he might have for young people; he replied thoughtfully, "I'm a great believer in what we have been told by people like [mythologist-] Joseph Campbell, 'Find your bliss.' Find out what touches you the most deeply. Pursue it, learn about it, explore it, expand on it.

Live with it and nurture it. Find your own way and make your own contribution."

Find your bliss. Find the route to your own happiness. If attending a convention helped put people on that path, if it added even a little joy to people's lives, then I was glad to be part of it. Admittedly, it took me some time to realize that and truly appreciate it. And I was equally glad to be paid to be part of it.

As the conventions got larger and larger, and the appearance fees increased, both Leonard and I began attending several of them a year. Because we had top billing, we were able to make demands. Just like rock stars! I insisted on hot tea, for example. And Leonard, Leonard was a lot tougher than I was. He demanded a pint of Häagen-Dazs coffee ice cream in his dressing room. Not mocha, not chocolate — coffee. And it had to be cold, and he had to have a spoon. This is the kind of thing that can happen when an actor gets too powerful! Often the very first thing he would do when he arrived at the venue was stalk into the green room, go to the food table, grab that ice cream, rip off the top, and start eating. After a couple of bites, he was ready to go. Perhaps the hardest part of doing the convention circuit was answering the same questions over and over with any type of enthusiasm. After a while, it became rote. The question asked most often to each of us was what our favorite episode was. No one would believe that was hard for me, but because I hadn't seen them all, I couldn't compare them. Most often I would respond that it was too hard to judge, but in fact I do have a soft spot for a wonderful story called "The Trouble with Tribbles." Leonard said he loved "The Devil in the Dark" episode, the "Amok Time" episode in which he created the salute and said "Live long and prosper" for the first time, and an episode written by the legendary writer Harlan Ellison, "The City on the Edge of Forever," in which crew members from the *Enterprise* go through a time warp and end up in New York City during the Depression. Leonard's least favorite episode, by the way, was our first show of the third season, "Spock's Brain." In this story, a beautiful alien woman gets on board the *Enterprise* and steals Spock's brain to save a civilization that needed it to control its power systems. Unfortunately, it turned Spock into a zombie, resulting in McCoy being forced to say what might have been the single worst line of the entire series, "Jim. His brain is gone!"

Putting on the ears was one thing, but

having to play a zombie? That part of Leonard's career had ended a long time earlier.

One night at a convention in Anaheim, Walter Koenig was answering the usual questions; by this time, he had all his pat answers and just pulled out the right one without having to think about it. That was true for all of us. But suddenly Walter found himself standing on stage, staring at the audience in total silence. Not one word was coming out of his mouth. He realized he had been skating through it without really paying any attention. He asked the fan to repeat the question, which was "If Chekov went to Disneyland, what would his favorite ride be?"

Thinking quickly, he responded, "Small World," because on this ride all the people of the planet were united.

The thing I disliked most about the conventions was signing hundreds and hundreds of autographs. I understood how important that was for the guests, but it was so impersonal. The whole object was to sign as many autographs as possible in the briefest time. We were told that the proper way to sign autographs is to never look up and make eye contact with an individual and never get involved in a conversation. The convention organizers made a considerable amount of their revenue from autographs and wanted us to sign every last one of them. It is highly organized: one person to one side slides the picture or book in front of us, we sign it without looking up, slide it to the person sitting on the other side who hands it to the fan, next.

I never really got very good at the not-looking-up part of it. I just couldn't help myself; I needed to look up and greet each person. I did get very good at the signing fast part, but nobody could top Leonard. Nobody. At one event, he was racing to finish so he could get to the airport and make his flight. The line was moving too slowly for him, so finally he got up from behind the table, went to each person in line, asked him or her to turn around, and then leaned on his or her back and signed the item. He signed his way to the end and then just kept going out the door and to the airport. They calculated he signed approximately 1,700 items in an hour, which has to stand as the all-time record.

While I came to enjoy attending these conventions, admittedly, I didn't completely grasp the appeal. It is difficult to find fault with being treated with total awe and respect, but inside it was impossible not to wonder if these people were seeing something in me that I didn't appreciate. In 1986, I was invited to host *Saturday Night Live.* By then, the concept of Trekkies was as well known as Grateful "Deadheads." In the opening skit written for me, I addressed the Trekkies, telling them, "Before I answer any more questions, there's something I wanted to say. Having receiving all of your letters over the years, and I've spoken to many of you, and some of you have traveled, y'know, hundreds of miles to be here, I'd just like to say . . . get a life, will you, people? I mean, for crying out loud, it's just a TV show . . .

"I mean, how old are you people? . . . [M]ove out of your parents' basements! And get your own apartments and grow the hell up! I mean, it's just a TV show, damn it. It's just a TV show."

It actually was intended to be a joke. And most Trekkies got the joke and began greeting each other by suggesting, "Get a life." But not everybody thought it was funny. It did not take long before I understood what Leonard had learned after titling his book *I Am Not Spock.* There are some people who took the mythology very seriously, perhaps too seriously. It actually was several years later, when I put on a mask and began interviewing people at conventions while working on a book and documentary aptly entitled *Get a Life* that I finally appreciated the fact that *Star Trek* was simply an escape from reality into a few moments of fantasy. And rather than being socially inept clichés as I had described them, Trekkies were instead, as Isaac Asimov said, "intelligent, interested, involved people with whom it is a pleasure to be, in any numbers. Why else would they have been involved in *Star Trek,* an intelligent, interested, and involved show?" And then he added, "Only once, in fact, did the general order and decorum break at one of these conventions, and that was when Mr. Spock (okay, Leonard Nimoy) made a brief appearance! And then the young women did do a little screaming!"

# EIGHT

It was these conventions that kept the franchise alive and led to the movies and the various TV series. For several years, we'd been hearing rumors that Paramount was considering reviving the series or producing a low-budget feature, but it never seemed to materialize. Finally, in 1975, they hired Roddenberry to write a screenplay. Typical of Roddenberry, he came up with an unexpected twist: the bad guy turned out to be God.

*Incubus* made more commercial sense.

Paramount then brought in Harlan Ellison, who created a story about the *Enterprise* time traveling back to the prehistoric era to save the future by fighting a race of giant reptiles. This was about the same time that *Chariots of the Gods,* a book by Erich von Däniken claiming that alien visitors had revealed their secrets to the ancient Mayans, was a huge sensation. During story meetings, a studio executive suggested Ellison add some Mayans to his concept. When Ellison explained patiently that in prehistoric times there were no Mayans, the executive said brightly, "Nobody'll know the difference!"

While the first *Star Trek* movie was in development, *Star Wars* was released. It became a worldwide sensation. Suddenly, there was a clamor for science fiction, and Paramount was uniquely positioned to take advantage of it. They had what was by now a proven show to drive right into that niche. Instead, they dropped the project.

About a year later, the studio announced it was going to boldly go where no one had gone before: it was going to start a fourth television network, and *Star Trek: Phase II* was going to be its first original series. Their problem was that Leonard didn't want to put the ears back on. Having been involved from the first pilot, he had spent more time aboard the *Enterprise* than any of us and just didn't want to do it anymore. His career was progressing comfortably, and he just wasn't interested. Additionally, he also was involved in a very complicated lawsuit with the studio about merchandising revenue. And his relationship with Roddenberry was almost nonexistent. During an argument,

Roddenberry had told him, "If it weren't for me, you wouldn't be who you are today!"

Whether it is accurate or not, it certainly wasn't the right thing to say to a man with great pride and talent who had earned everything he'd gotten in the business. Leonard responded, "Don't do me any more other favors." So when his agent called to tell him about the offer, he supposedly responded, "If you ever call me again about *Star Trek,* you're fired."

The concept of making *Star Trek* without Spock was like making *My Fair Lady* without Eliza Doolittle — the dance numbers were going to be very awkward. I didn't try to talk him into it. Leonard did not make decisions rashly; they were well thought out, and once made, he did not easily change his mind. Finally, the studio offered Leonard a good deal to appear in a minimum of two episodes out of every eleven that were shot. Paramount added some new characters, including another Vulcan, and was in pre-production when *Close Encounters of the Third Kind* was released and began breaking box office records.

The series idea was dropped. Almost instantly, the goal became a movie. They changed the sets, they changed the costumes, and they brought in director Robert

Wise, who had won Academy Awards for both *The Sound of Music* and *West Side Story.* He also had directed the 1951 science-fiction movie *The Day the Earth Stood Still,* which was probably why the studio hired him. The problem was that Wise had never seen an episode of the show and didn't seem to understand its appeal. His wife and his father-in-law were big fans, though, and made it clear to him that without Spock there was no *Star Trek.* Leonard finally had Hollywood clout. They needed him desperately. Leonard was starring in *Equus* on Broadway, and Paramount executive Jeffrey Katzenberg flew to New York to meet with him. Leonard held his ground against a man recognized as one of the best negotiators in the industry; he would not agree to appear in the movie until his lawsuit was settled.

The lawsuit was settled within a few weeks. An hour after Leonard received his check, he got a copy of the script. We also negotiated very good deals for this movie; at that time, nobody truly appreciated the real value of this franchise. Leonard and I received a very good payout from Paramount based on a rather obtuse phrase my attorney found in our contracts.

The problem was that the studio didn't

have a story to tell. We started filming without a completed script and would get new pages every day, sometimes several times a day. The script was ponderous; perhaps to save money, it was all talk and very little action. Maybe some studio executive should have realized that in Wise's previous science film the earth had stood still. It didn't move at all. That was the problem with our script.

It was the amazing special effects — in addition to the wonderful stories — that had made both *Star Wars* and *Close Encounters* such huge hits. But we ended up with a lot of grand ideas that most often didn't make a lot of sense. There was no suspense, no intrigue, no buildup, so there was no real climax. I mean, literally, there was no climax; no one had figured out the ending of the film. Most importantly, though, the tone was all wrong. Wise didn't get it. I remember when we were rehearsing the first scene, in which Kirk was thanking the members of the crew for coming out of retirement to save the universe. In fact, this was setting up the sequel. Kirk told Dee Kelley's McCoy, "I'll have you back to Earth shortly," to which he replied, "Oh, Captain, I might as well stay."

Kirk turned to Spock and told him, "I'll

take you back to Vulcan."

The line in the script was perfunctory and bland. Leonard ad-libbed the perfect answer, "Captain, if Dr. McCoy is to remain on board, my presence here will be essential."

It was a line that accurately described the relationship between Spock and Bones, a line that would cause every fan to smile knowingly — but Wise didn't get it at all. Instead, he told us, "You know, the feeling is that the humor is inappropriate."

*Thud.* Leonard and I realized if this project was going to be as good as we all wanted it to be, we had to get involved. We began spending a lot of time together in our dressing rooms, more time than we'd ever spent together, trying to find ways to bring the movie alive. We struggled with it, but we were able to come up with some pretty decent concepts, and several of them did make it into the movie. To add action, for example, Kirk discovered Spock's spacesuit was missing and realized Spock had set out on his own, so Kirk put on his own suit and chased Spock through space. To Wise's credit, he was open to suggestions. Once, though, we came up with a wonderful idea for a big action event to set up the climax. It was brilliant — I'm absolutely certain of that — even if I don't remember the details. Like the idea. We went together to Wise and told it to him. He liked it, but it would be expensive, and he didn't have the authority to make those changes.

Roddenberry did. Roddenberry was the producer and credited as one of the writers. He had approved everything we disliked so much. He had a limited amount of money to spend. Convincing him to make this change was a significant challenge, and we both knew it. But we were up to the task. We believed it was absolutely necessary. So we spent all afternoon together rehearsing our pitch. We acted it out several times. When we went into Gene's office early in the evening, we were primed.

Roddenberry sat there listening. There was something terribly intimidating about telling him what had to be done to save his script. As we went through our concept, it seemed to have lost all its energy. It didn't sound as good in Roddenberry's office as it had in Wise's office. It fell totally flat. When we were done, we sort of skulked out of his office.

Leonard and I laughed about that for the rest of our lives together. I think we both understood and accepted, maybe for the first time, that we truly were bound together by this amazing adventure we were cast into. No one would ever understand it, both the joys and the problems, better than the two of us. We established a new comfort level with each other.

The final picture was considerably less than the combined level of experience and creativity that went into making it. I don't think anybody had realized how hard it was going to be updating the show while retaining its feel. Very little had been thought out. The new uniforms we wore, for example, looked good but were very poorly designed. Essentially, they were made from skintight spandex, and they were very uncomfortable. Most distressing, they didn't have a fly in front, as if by the twenty-third century mankind had discovered a way to avoid going to the bathroom. The outfit was zipped on and off — and the zipper was in the back, so when we took a restroom break, we had to be accompanied by someone from the costume department. When the production crew tested the transporter for the first time, the lights on the lighted platform generated so much heat that the rubber soles of their shoes melted.

The original budget was $15 million, which actually was a substantial budget in 1977. But with all the problems that had to be solved and the semi-special effects that had to be added weeks before the scheduled release date, the picture cost $46 million to produce, at that time making it the second-most expensive Hollywood film ever made. A lot of studio executives resumed breathing when the film opened in December 1979; it set a record for the highest weekend gross, proving that fans would turn out to see it. While the reviews were reasonable, the picture earned almost $140 million.

Leonard's relationship with Spock was always ambivalent. He appreciated what Spock had done for his career, but he also was determined to prove that he was a lot more than a Vulcan. There was no doubt it caused an identity crisis. He really had to choose whether to embrace Spock completely or fight this wave of love for the character. What he eventually came to realize was that he had no choice; he had brought to life a unique character that millions of people had embraced deeply and were not about to easily let go. At times, it got really silly. When news leaked that Spock was going to die in *Star Trek II,* director Nick Meyer got a letter threatening, "If Spock dies, you die." For whatever reasons, maybe because Jim Kirk looked a lot like me, that problem did not affect me nearly as deeply.

We talked about the relationship between an actor and the character, and there never was a doubt in my mind that Leonard was proud of his creation and had real affection for Spock, but he didn't want to be weighed down by it. Leonard spent his life always moving forward, doing the next thing. Even as his body began failing later in his life, his mind continued to race forward, planning the next project. Harve Bennett, who produced the second *Star Trek* movie, *The Wrath of Khan,* once said, "I never understood why Leonard became an actor, he is pure intellect . . . Very bright, very gifted, and there is something about his non-acting that makes him an authority figure. You put ears on him and it all came together."

The putting-the-ears-on-him part was the problem when Paramount decided to move forward with the second movie. Leonard just didn't want to do it. It was Bennett's task to convince him to join the cast one more time. A rumor started somewhere that as a condition of appearing in the movie, Leonard demanded a clause in his contract that Spock would die in the movie. The people that heard that assumed that was his way of burying Spock forever. The problem was that it wasn't true. In fact, not only wasn't it true, it made Leonard furious. He actually wrote a letter to the *Star Trek* fan magazine, stating flatly, "You report that the death of Spock was 'brought about by Leonard Nimoy's request.' In your January issue you reiterated the same report and then you quoted *Star Trek II* executive producer Harve Bennett as saying, 'Nimoy did not insist on killing the character as a prerequisite to his appearing in the second film.' I was not contacted for a statement but here it is: Harve Bennett was right, you were wrong . . . twice! Yours for more accurate journalism."

It was Bennett who talked him into it, telling him, "I'm gonna give you the greatest death scene in motion pictures." Why not? Leonard agreed, "If this was going to be the end of *Star Trek,* let's go out in a blaze of glory, saving the *Enterprise.* Dying a hero." And it is possible he believed that after this movie, he finally was going to free of Spock.

I actually helped write Spock's death scene. We were in Harve Bennett's office, and he was outlining his vision of the scene. I suggested that it would be cinematic to have us separated by the plate-glass door, while our hands were seemingly touching each other.

Nick Meyer waited until almost the very

end before shooting Spock's death scene. It turned out to be an emotional day, one even I was not truly prepared for. As far as all of us who had been on this journey almost from the beginning were concerned, there was a real sense of finality. This was the end of Spock. But perhaps the most surprised at those feelings was Leonard. I have read stories from other people that he was unusually tense that day, but I don't remember that. I think we all were wound up in our own feelings. During the filming of that scene, there were a lot of real tears shed for our fictional friend. But what Leonard said later was that even he was not as prepared for Spock's death as he thought he would be. He remembers thinking as he walked onto the set, "I think I have made a terrible mistake."

What saved him, he said, was that as we got ready to film the scene, Bennett asked him if there was something he could add that would give the studio a thread that might be used to keep Spock alive.

Alive? Nick Meyer acknowledged that we all knew our characters better than he did, so there was quite a bit of adlibbing. And Leonard gave them the thread they needed: "Remember."

If Leonard and Harve Bennett had agreed

on a plan that could be used to bring Spock back to life in a later movie, I knew nothing about it. As far as I believed, this was the end of Spock, and in this scene, I was saying good-bye to an extraordinary being.

Shooting that scene was very meaningful to both Leonard and me. We both treasured it. The scene played on a lot of levels, the obvious one being a climactic scene in a good movie. More than that, though, both of us were beginning to become aware of our own mortality. We were at that point in the aging process where suddenly you become aware of the fragility of life. While neither one of us was ill, our children were grown, and we were moving into the next stage of life. So there was a great deal of feeling as we looked at each other through that glass, a great deal. We both recognized the elements of real life on that soundstage that day.

The *Wrath of Khan* set new box office records for an opening weekend and received wonderful reviews. But rather than being the end of Spock, the success of the movie saved the franchise.

# NINE

With all the acclaim that Leonard received for his work on the original series, with all the emotional conflicts that he endured about the creation of this big-eared alter ego that occupied such a large space in his world, he once summed up very simply and directly what Spock meant to him: "He gave me a life."

The third season was difficult for all of us because the quality of the show had deteriorated, and we knew it. So we all were glad when it ended. Of all of us, though, it was Leonard whose life had changed the most drastically because of *Star Trek*. When it ended, he had several options, and one of them he picked was so perfectly Leonard: he became co-owner of Leonard Nimoy's Pet Pad. It was a pet store in Canoga Park in the San Fernando Valley that carried a great variety of exotic pets, including monkeys, snakes, crocodiles, and exotic dogs and cats. "I like the kind of people that shop in pet stores," he told a reporter, adding that he had worked in a pet store between roles earlier in his career. And then he admitted that he had invested in the shop as "a sort of therapy, something to keep me busy."

That was so typical of Leonard. Like Spock, I suppose, his mind was constantly searching for the next challenge. Most people, when you ask them what's new, respond in a somewhat predictable fashion. It may be bigger and better, but it's most often an extension of what they have been doing for some time. Not Leonard. When I asked him that question, I never knew where he may have been exploring. In addition to the pet store, for example, he and Sandi had moved into a new home, and he'd bought her an electric kiln for her ceramic work. But he'd also gotten interested in it and began creating glazes for her finished pieces.

There were several traits that Leonard and I had in common, and certainly one of them was our curiosity. Neither one of us ever stopped asking why, or how, or learning new things. When we were intrigued about something, we would dive into something, and neither one of us would stop until we had conquered it. For example, I had my private pilot license and sang the praises of flying. Not too long after that, he too became a pilot, but a much better one than I. He became quite good at it and even had his own airplane, a single-engine Piper Arrow. He'd often fly his son, Adam, back and forth to college in Santa Barbara, and he would bring the same intensity to flying as he did to everything else in his life. "He was a highly competent pilot," Adam said. "Like everything else, he was kind of obsessive about it. He earned his instrument rating. When he was flying, he was totally focused. There was nothing casual about it; while he always was very confident and comfortable, you couldn't talk to him too much. He brought all his attention to what he was doing."

That obsessive aspect of his personality became pretty clear when he was talking about soloing for the first time. He was in London making a television movie, and he remembered, "I was so busy thinking about what I was doing that it took me a while to realize that there was nobody else in the plane. It wasn't until I was almost finished with the downwind leg and about to turn on base when I took a look around and said, 'My God, I'm alone.'" Typical, so typical.

I flew with him on occasion. For a time, he had a house on Lake Tahoe, and we would take his plane to get there. It's not an easy place to land. The lake is surrounded by high mountains, so instead of making a normal approach, you have to circle down into the valley and land. It requires a certain level of expertise. On one of those trips, we flew through a storm, and the plane was hit by lightning. There was a bright flash and a loud thump. In fact, we were not in danger, because planes are designed to take this kind of blow. But it definitely was unnerving. Neither one of us said a word; we looked at each other and acknowledged the possibility of what could have happened: Captain Kirk and Mr. Spock, having flown through the universe on a great spaceship, having survived numerous encounters with the worst beings in existence, went down together in a small single-engine airplane.

Leonard also became more visible for those causes he supported. This was the 1960s, a tumultuous period in American history. As a Canadian citizen living and working in the United States, I really didn't believe I had the right to participate in American political issues. But Sandi was an activist, and Leonard just jumped right in with her to support their beliefs. They were shaken by the assassination of Martin Luther King Jr. in May 1968, and Leonard spear-headed a food drive for Dr. King's Poor People's Campaign, then joined people like Jack Lemmon and Barbra Streisand at a benefit at the Hollywood Bowl that drew eighteen thousand people and raised $142,000. He also volunteered a lot of his time emceeing local telethons for a variety of good charities, including United Cerebral Palsy, the March of Dimes, and Variety Clubs. They both got involved in the antiwar campaigns of both Eugene McCarthy in 1968 and George McGovern four years later. Leonard visited thirty-five states during the McGovern campaign. When he was up in Alaska, a TV reporter asked him if he thought it was appropriate for a television star to use his celebrity to influence voters. Once again, I can hear him responding as if the answer was obvious: "Well, I think it's about as fair as Ronald Reagan running for governor of California based on the fact that he's done some movies."

Leonard campaigned for McGovern anywhere people would listen to him, from large rallies in arenas to talking to a few committed young people in a college dorm. As always, his message was one of compassion. He was supporting Senator McGovern, he told 350 people in Toledo, Ohio, because he had promised to end the war in Vietnam, and the millions of dollars that would be saved could be spent "to build homes and hospitals and finance ecology programs."

Leonard's passionate support made absolutely no difference. Nixon won forty-nine of the fifty states in a landslide. In appreciation of Leonard's support, however, McGovern read several of his poems into the Congressional Record.

At a rally sponsored by the American Civil Liberties Union, he was introduced to Dr. Benjamin Spock, the legendary author of *Baby and Child Care,* whose involvement in the anti–Vietnam War movement had led to him being arrested several times for interfering with draft board activities. This was the only time the two most famous Spocks in the world ever met, and while the two men were never mistaken for each other, *Star Trek*'s Mr. Spock had on occasion been referred to as Dr. Spock. When the two men met, Leonard said, "How do you do? My name is Leonard Nimoy, and I play a character called Mr. Spock on television."

Dr. Spock looked at him, smiled, and

replied, "I know. Have you been indicted yet?"

Leonard's active involvement in causes in which he believed never waned. We both knew the publicity value of Kirk and Spock appearing together, so we used it judiciously to benefit those organizations in which we truly believed. If I needed him to show up at one of my charity events, I'd make the call, knowing that he would do exactly the same thing. Except for scheduling conflicts, I don't think either one of us ever turned down a request — but because we both knew we didn't really have a choice, we limited the number of requests.

*Star Trek* provided his fame, but the first substantial money he earned came from *Mission: Impossible.* Everybody knows the *Mission: Impossible* setup: To save the world or rescue an extremely important person or prevent a coup, the MI team has to create an unbelievably clever deception to make someone do something they don't want to do, usually without them knowing they're doing it: Paris poses as an amnesia victim to retrieve the stolen isotope that could make atomic weapons affordable to every country in the world; Paris plays a mystic who plans to abuse his powerful influence over a duchess to ascend to the throne; Paris impersonates an American mobster in order to infiltrate the Syndicate's Mediterranean branch, obtain the list of their opium suppliers, and prevent the branch's terminally ill boss from perpetuating his empire.

Leonard was paid $7,500 a week, a substantial salary in 1969. In addition to that salary, for the first time he began earning residuals. With a hit show like that certain to run for a long time in syndication, that was like putting money in the bank. *Mission: Impossible* was a success when he joined the cast and continued to be successful after he left two years later. I think he joined the show for several different reasons; like all of us, I know he worried about being so typecast that he would find it difficult to get other roles. Maybe just as importantly, this role offered him the opportunity to join a strong cast that was not dependent on him. And the fact that in the role of ex-magician, master of disguises Andrew "the Great" Paris he would get to play a variety of different characters I'm sure appealed to his description of himself as a character actor.

In his first episode, he got to put on a beret and a beard, smoke a big cigar, and play a Che Guevara–type character. That certainly was a departure from three seasons of life in space, as I don't recall Spock wearing a beard or smoking a cigar — although undoubtedly he would have found the cigar "fascinating." Initially, Leonard enjoyed doing the show; it allowed him more freedom to play than he'd had in a while. But that didn't last long. After two years, he found himself doing it mostly for the salary. Unlike Spock, whose life story emerged slowly as the series continued, Paris just existed. He had no backstory. It didn't matter where he came from, what issues he faced in his life, or how he would deal with them. For an actor in love with his craft, it was like playing a cardboard box. There was no sense of continuity in the role, no internal life, no emotional core from which everything could flow. All he had to do was show up, put on the disguise of the week, and convince the bad guys he was whoever he had become in that episode. And then he found himself playing the same shallow roles more than once. He was the Latin American dictator, he was the very old man, he was blind, he was Japanese, he was an old blind Japanese dictator. It was "throw on the makeup and read the lines."

After two seasons, he decided it was time to leave. His reason, he explained, was that he had reached "professional menopause."

It was time for an artistic change of life . . .

"It was a great job. They treated me great, paid me a lot of money, and the hours were easy. But I'd done five steady years of television. I thought, that's enough for a while. I made enough money to last me a long time. I'll have good residuals coming in for several years, and I might as well go out and act in other areas now . . .

"If I could get a play somewhere, I should go out and do it and just start getting back to being an actor again."

Fame changes people. It does — it can't be helped. I've seen it so many times in my career. I've seen people use it as a ladder to better roles; I've seen careers destroyed by it. I don't think people really can predict how they will react if they catch that particular gold ring. Leonard never loved being famous, although he enjoyed the accoutrements that came with success. At times, as we all do, he found the constant attention overwhelming; he never liked the fact that he simply couldn't sit in a restaurant with his family or some friends without being interrupted. Generally, he was good about it, though; he gave autographs and posed for pictures, but he was wary of the stalkers, the people who found out when his plane was arriving at an airport and followed him.

I think what kept Leonard from ever fully embracing his fame was the fact that he considered himself a working actor and considered that about the best thing in the world anybody could be. He'd set out to make a living at it, never expecting to become a star. But even after he did, his passion for the profession of acting never diminished. He loved talking about it, thinking about it, teaching it, and doing it. He loved taking this unformed lump of written lines and converting it into a vehicle capable of evoking great emotion. I just think he was always curious to see the result of the creative process. He explained the process this way: "My job is to be part of the magical illusion created equally by the play, the players, and the audience. When all those elements meet in the right way, the truth takes place between us and within us, and it's an experience like no other I know."

Nowhere is an actor more alive than on stage, when he or she is receiving an immediate and direct response from the audience. Making movies or TV shows is a different process; it's working in pieces and most often not in any kind of order. There are times when it makes sense to film the dramatic conclusion at the very beginning.

But the theater . . . it's different.

After leaving *M:I,* Leonard became a gypsy actor, touring the country in several different plays. His name always packed the theater, and he played roles as varied as Tevye in *Fiddler on the Roof* to the controversial businessman Goldman in *The Man in the Glass Booth.* Tevye the singing milkman in *Fiddler* hardly is the first role you'd associate with Leonard — but it was a part he really wanted to play. While people had become accustomed to seeing large, bold, loud men like Zero Mostel in the role of the milkman whose family is forced to leave their ancestral village, it actually fit Leonard well. He easily related his own family background to Tevye; this story was his heritage, and he embraced it. The strength in his performance was his ability to channel his own experience into Tevye's, and what his singing voice may have lacked in quality was infused with his passion and understanding. I tell a joke during a one-man show I do about a record company named Golden Throat who took every actor who thought he or she could sing and put all those songs into an album entitled *Golden Throats: The Great Celebrity Sing-Off.* In addition to Leonard and me, some of the other performers included Andy Griffith, Jim Nabors, Mae West, and Jack Webb. While to many people Mae West's version of "Twist and Shout" is a highlight, the only two performers with more than one cut on the record were Leonard and I. Leonard performed "If I Had a Hammer" and "Proud Mary" while I did my rendition of "Lucy in the Sky with Diamonds" and "Mr. Tambourine Man." In fact, Leonard actually could carry a tune while I could carry the guitar case.

At one point, he did *Fiddler* at the Wilbur Theater in downtown Boston, which finally allowed his parents to see him on stage. He used to laugh about the fact that his mother and father never quite understood *Star Trek* and certainly didn't understand Spock — but at least he was working. And he was kind enough not to remind his father that he had never taken an accordion lesson. His parents knew something special was going on; apparently, young kids would come into his father's barbershop and ask for a haircut like Spock's. What his parents did understand was that he had married a nice Jewish girl and was earning a living at the acting. But Tevye? Tevye they understood.

It was an odd juxtaposition indeed moving from *Fiddler* to Robert Shaw's *The Man in the Glass Booth*. This was a highly controversial, provocative drama dealing with Jewish guilt. Oy. There's a difficult subject. Based very loosely on the trial of Adolf Eichmann, it's the story of a concentration camp survivor who becomes a very successful New York businessman and then somehow convinces the Israelis to put him on trial as a war criminal. At the conclusion of the trial, he locks himself into the glass booth meant to protect him in the courtroom and has a long monologue about the meaning of Hitler to the Germans. It's an extraordinarily chilling moment of theater, "People of Israel," he begins. "People of Israel. If he had chosen you . . . if he had chosen you . . . you also would have followed where he led." When the play was done on Broadway starring Donald Pleasence, at its conclusion each night, some people in the audience literally would throw things at the stage.

Leonard did it first at the Old Globe Theatre in San Diego soon after finishing shooting *M:I*. His pay was $300 a week, which was not sufficient to cover his expenses. But as he said, "What made it worthwhile was that this was a case of knowing what I was doing and why I was doing it." While the theater sold out and Leonard received a standing ovation every night, there were some people in the San Diego Jewish community who believed the play was anti-Semitic. Leonard actually organized a seminar at a local temple to discuss the play, and I absolutely know Leonard must have been in heaven about that. This was the kind of response to theater, to acting, that made him love this world.

One of the complaints that came up during the meeting was that the portrayal of the central character as a Jew who had succeeded through real estate and financial manipulation was based on anti-Semitic stereotypes. Leonard described the exchange of ideas at that meeting as "lively." I can just imagine what went on, but I know for certain he was in the middle of it, sparking ideas, questions, and challenges.

It actually is somewhat unusual for the theater to break the fourth wall and respond to the action on the stage. It happened to Leonard on another occasion, when he was playing the title role, another immortal character, in the Royal Shakespeare Company's national tour of *Sherlock Holmes*. He actually was physically perfect for the role, angular and lean, somewhat darkish in nature, equipped with inquisitive eyes and a somber voice. Years earlier, Roddenberry had briefly pursued a couple of Holmes projects for him, but it never developed. An afternoon matinee in Detroit's Fisher Theatre was filled with Trekkies who had come to see the sleuth at work. *Laugh-In*'s Alan Sues played Holmes's mortal enemy, the evil Moriarty. In the somewhat stirring conclusion, to the surprise of absolutely no one, Leonard's Holmes makes a brilliant deduction and arrests Moriarty. As he is being dragged offstage to the hoosegow, Moriarty turned and screamed his warning at Holmes, "Wherever you go, I will be there, and when I fall, you'll fall with me!"

At that, a woman sitting near the front stood up and — to great cheers — responded, "Oh no you won't! Because you're a crook, and you'll make a mistake!"

Leonard's performance in *Fiddler* led him to be cast in several other touring musicals; he played Fagin in *Oliver,* King Arthur in *Camelot,* and even Professor Henry Higgins in *My Fair Lady.* Both Leonard and I always had an initial hurdle to overcome when we did live theater: a sizeable number of people in the audience had come to see Captain Kirk and Mr. Spock in the flesh. They had to lay aside all their preconceptions to accept either of us in a different role. We knew we had been successful when people walked out of the theater admitting that for a few minutes, at least, they forgot it was really Captain Kirk or Mr. Spock up there. And that was a great victory.

One of those people who was convinced Leonard could shed his ears was the great movie director Otto Preminger, who saw him as King Arthur and cast him into the Broadway play he was producing in 1973 entitled *Full Circle*. This was Leonard's debut on Broadway, a dream come true. It was based on a film cowritten by pacifist Erich Maria Remarque, who was famous for the World War I saga *All Quiet on the Western Front,* entitled *The Last Ten Days,* and it was adapted for the American stage by Peter Stone. It was essentially an antiwar play, which obviously was perfect for Leonard. It was a one act costarring Swedish actress Bibi Andersson and took place in a small room in Berlin at the end of World War II. Leonard played an escaped political prisoner who, while disguised as a Nazi, is captured by the Russians.

Working with the famous, pompous Preminger was not an especially good experience. As a director, Leonard was very sympathetic to actors; Preminger was not. Leonard once said that Preminger's entire directing technique consisted of yelling at the actors in his thick German accent, "Ze lines! You must learn ze lines!"

After rehearsal one night, Leonard stopped into a bar to relax. The Spock mystique was at full attraction, and a woman began a conversation, which ended very quickly when she invited him back to her apartment. It just wasn't something he wanted to do. But rather than hurting her feelings, he told her truthfully that he had to go back to his hotel room and learn his lines. The next few days' rehearsals apparently did not go well, and Preminger started screaming. Leonard always was prepared; he always knew his lines. And he stood up to Preminger and told him the whole story. Preminger considered that, then decided, "For ze lines you learned, you shudda screwed her!"

*Full Circle* ran twenty-eight performances and closed. The range of plays in which Leonard starred covered pretty much the whole spectrum of American theater, from serious dramas like *The Man in the Glass Booth* and *Full Circle* to many of the great exuberant musicals to light comedies like *6 Rms Riv Vu* opposite Sandy Dennis and even the heartbreaking comedy *One Flew Over the Cuckoo's Nest*. But the play that was most meaningful to him undoubtedly was the one he wrote, *Vincent,* the story of Van Gogh as told mostly through letters he had written to his beloved brother Theo.

Nobody ever claimed Leonard chose to do the easy thing. For a time after *Star Trek,* he supplemented his income visiting college campuses to talk about the show. He was a big hit with students, and the money was good. After only a few years, though, he said, "I felt repetitive and, as is my nature, I began searching for a new challenge." His plan was to develop a one-person show that he could tour with that both satisfied his curiosity and allowed him to continue acting. After being part of an ensemble like the crew of the starship *Enterprise,* he wanted to find a vehicle that would allow him to be on stage, alone. And, of course, one that continued to pay well.

After speaking at a college in upstate New York, he accepted a dinner invitation from members of the faculty. During the discussion that night, he asked about other lecturers they'd had. Earlier that year, he learned, an actor had performed a one-man show called *Van Gogh* written by Phillip Stevens. It was the story of Vincent van Gogh as told by his brother Theo, who loved and supported him emotionally and financially.

It's not difficult to figure out what attracted Leonard to this story. As he once told an interviewer while promoting it, "Vincent struggled for twenty years to find himself. And then he found his art." In essence, it was a story of unbridled artistic passion. "I have a tremendous identification with Vincent," he admitted before another performance. "Like him, I really believe I have something to offer, and that I really want to give it."

Leonard bought the rights to the play from Stevens and began slowly rewriting it. During his research, he discovered a letter Theo had written to his infirm mother after Vincent's death, describing his funeral. Vincent and Theo had written more than five hundred letters over a ten-year period, and these letters told a wonderful story, describing in detail Vincent's struggles to create and his small victories. Leonard understood that through these letters it was possible to tell a story of artistic creation that anyone with their own passion might understand and relate to. "If a poet touches your soul," read one of the letters, "he gives you a sense of universal connection with the rest of the universe.

"Must he have proper table manners as well?"

The structure is a simple one. The play

takes place a week after Vincent's death, and Theo has invited several of his friends to hear him make his own statement about his seemingly misunderstood brother, which he does by reading from their correspondence. And a moment near the end of the first segment probably makes the statement Leonard wanted to make with this show: "Vincent, love your whore, love nature, love life, love that bastard Gauguin, but for God's sake, Vincent, learn to love yourself!"

After several tryouts in Sacramento in 1978, Leonard did the show for the first time at the Tyrone Guthrie Theater, a prestigious regional theater in Minneapolis. The reviews for *Vincent* were terrific, and Leonard presented the show hundreds of times in cities all across America. While the show was written to use locally available props to make it easy to transport, it grew to be a two thousand–pound set that Leonard would pack up and store in his garage in Bel Air. The show eventually became his actor's security blanket. No matter how successful an actor might be, at some point, in the dark of the night, way back in the recesses of his or her mind, he or she wonders and fears that it's all going to fall apart. Very few actors are immune to that. So what some actors do is find a vehicle, a one-man show that they can always go on tour with and make a few bucks. Hal Holbrook's *Mark Twain Tonight!* James Whitmore's *Will Rogers' USA.* Tony Lo Bianco as Fiorello LaGuardia in *The Little Flower.*

French actor Jean-Michel Richaud discovered the play in 2011 and wanted to play the role. He and Leonard became friends, and as Jean-Michel remembers, "When we would talk about it, he would go to the edge of the seat and move forward. He would become very animated and, for sure, there was a twinkle in his eye. He would tell me that the play was pulling at him. Many times he would put it to rest, and from time to time, he would hear the furniture set in his garage calling to him."

Leonard actually found a clever way to support his research into Van Gogh's life. In 1976, producer Alan Landsburg had hired him to narrate his series entitled *In Search Of . . .* which investigated mysterious phenomena. Landsburg successfully made several documentaries, including *In Search of Ancient Astronauts* and *In Search of Ancient Mysteries,* which had been narrated by Rod Serling. After Serling's death in 1975, Landsburg needed someone to replace him, and Leonard's great popularity with science-fiction fans made him the perfect choice. It almost didn't happen. Leonard had done the pilot episode for a somewhat similar show entitled *The Unexplained*. In that episode, Leonard interviewed a young man who claimed to have been abducted by aliens — the perfect show for Spock. But when that show was not bought, Landsburg hired him immediately.

This was the kind of job every actor loves. Almost all the work is done by other people, and you just show up for a day or two to tape voiceovers or do an entrance and exit. It's often possible to film several shows in one day. It allows an actor to earn a good salary while still having time to work on those projects that really interest him. During one period, for example, Leonard was starring in *Equus* on Broadway. Every few weeks, Landsburg would send a film crew to New York; and on the day the show was dark, they would race around the city finding appropriate backgrounds for Leonard do his intros and exits. They filmed in graveyards, in old brownstones; they did the introduction to a show about Native American faith in the National Museum of the American Indian. The next morning, he'd go into a recording studio and do the narrations.

The good news for Leonard was that this

was an interesting show, often investigating subjects that probably intrigued him, including the Abominable Snowman, ghosts, voodoo, the Shroud of Turin, mummies, the disappearance of bandleader Glenn Miller, and life before birth, although it also treated some questionable subjects, like killer bees, alien abductions, and the Amityville Horror, with equal respect. Leonard was particularly curious about those things that seemed just a little bit beyond our knowledge, things like ESP, hypnosis, and supernatural phenomena. While Leonard was writing *Vincent,* he was able to convince Landsburg to send him to Europe to research and write an episode for the show . . . "In Search of Vincent van Gogh."

During his research, Leonard was able to visit those places Van Gogh had lived and painted in France and Holland. In fact, while digging into Van Gogh's life, he actually discovered some hospital records that indicated the painter had suffered from epilepsy rather than being insane.

*In Search Of . . .* was the perfect show for Leonard to host, because more than anyone I have ever known, Leonard spent his entire life in search of knowledge and creative expression.

# TEN

Before *Star Trek,* producers were hiring a respected character actor when they called him; after *Star Trek* they wanted his name, although most of the time his full name was usually "*Star Trek*'s Leonard Nimoy." But now people knew it, and it attracted a growing audience. It was an odd time for Leonard — the first time in his career he had the luxury of making choices rather than accepting roles for the income. The actor's inclination always is to say yes and then feel relieved he or she has a job. Leonard was carefully feeling his way into his post-Spock career. He made several mostly forgettable films. What he was really trying to do was shed his ears. Instead, what he was discovering, as I did, was that there was no such thing as post–*Star Trek.* In almost every story or review about whatever it was he was doing, almost inevitably there would be a reference or a comparison to Spock. "Tevye is not recognizable as Spock" or his character in the remake of *Invasion of the Body Snatchers* "is the evil side of Spock." I've wondered if reporters or critics ever realized when they wrote that he had successfully made the audience forget Spock for a few hours that they actually were pointing out that no one had really forgotten about Spock.

Forgotten? In fact, the opposite was true. While each member of the original cast was finding his or her own projects, in the background, *Star Trek* was growing more popular in syndication than it had ever been during its original run. Rather than successfully escaping it, it was overtaking and enveloping all of us. It was as if it had become the theme music of our lives.

Soon after Leonard quit *M:I,* he accepted his very first starring role in a television movie, an *ABC Movie of the Week* thriller called *Assault on the Wayne.* He played the commander of a nuclear submarine carrying a secret antimissile weapon. As he discovers his crew has been infiltrated by enemy agents who intend to sail the sub into a mid-ocean trap and steal the device, Commander Kettenring has to somehow figure out which members of his crew are traitors to foil their plot. Unfortunately, the movie sank, although it still shows up on occasion on late-night television.

Following that, he made several films, including his first theatrical feature, the cowboy movie *Catlow* in which — just like the days before *Star Trek* — he played the villain. He costarred with Yul Brynner and Richard Crenna while his friend and mentor Jeff Corey also had a small role.

It was a bumpy road, filled with plays, TV movies, and one-shots in popular series. I was following the same path. The phone rang a lot, but as much as we pretended it wasn't true, we were both carrying our characters on our backs.

Leonard made some interesting choices, among them starring in his first major Hollywood film, director Philip Kaufman's remake of the suspense classic *The Invasion of the Body Snatchers.* Donald Sutherland and Jeff Goldblum costarred with him, and Robert Duvall made an unbilled cameo as a priest on a swing. In this story, aliens have come from outer space to colonize Earth. They arrived as giant seedpods that are hidden under beds, and when a human goes to sleep, an exact replica emerges from the pod and takes control of his or her body. Physically, they are exact duplicates, but they have no emotional center; they are completely dispassionate.

Dispassionate aliens? Now that sounds familiar. I wonder why they thought of Leonard.

In the film, he plays a psychiatrist and the author of several bestselling self-help books who refuses to believe claims made by friends that people they love have changed somehow, that they have lost access to their emotions. Leonard's Dr. Kibner listens sympathetically but implores these people to be rational. In soft and measured tones, he manages to calm their fear — then the audience discovers that he is one of the pod people. In fact, he may well be the leader of the invasion. One critic pointed out the greatest irony — none of Dr. Kibner's close friends, the people who come to him for help, even notice that he himself is devoid of emotion.

In some ways, this is Leonard showing Spock's dark side, an alien unable to experience any of the human emotions that Spock always found so fascinating yet also was unable to feel.

I'm not sure when each member of the original cast accepted the inevitable, that we were bound to *Star Trek* forever. I know I probably resisted longer than anyone else. I still kind of thought my most memorable role was around the next corner. It took me quite a while to understand and finally appreciate and be very grateful for the important place that Kirk and the crew of the *Enterprise* filled in the entertainment universe.

It was while Leonard was working on *Body Snatchers* that Paramount decided to go ahead with the first *Star Trek* movie. Only after they settled his lawsuit for a percentage of merchandising revenue did he agree to appear in it. With the success of that film, the studio was finally beginning to understand the potential value of this property. This TV show that had struggled through three seasons had become a franchise. Paramount immediately began planning a second *Star Trek* feature. Leonard agreed to do it — we all did — but this time he demanded a guarantee from the studio that they would find other, very different roles for him. The studio agreed to two "pay or play" commitments. They would have to pay him for two more films, whether or not they used him. I know studios; if they were paying him, they would find a way to use him.

While the script for *Star Trek II* was being written, he accepted the role of the Israeli pioneer and Prime Minister Golda Meir's husband, Morris Meyerson, in the TV movie *A Woman Called Golda.* Initially, he turned it down, not sure he could do it, but the producer finally talked him into it. In the movie, which was filmed in Israel, the great actresses Judy Davis and Ingrid Bergman played Golda at different times of her life. This was only a few years after the miniseries *Roots* had caused people to start searching for their own heritage, and with roles like Tevye and Meyerson, it was as if Leonard was exploring his Jewish roots. Working with Ingrid Bergman was especially poignant for him. While making this film, she was dying of cancer, and everyone in the cast and crew knew it. Leonard remembers how wardrobe created costumes to keep her arm, badly swollen arm from the treatments she was receiving, covered. He spoke to her for the last time several months after the film was done. She had stopped taking her medication, she said. It made her feel awful, and she accepted that whatever was going to happen would happen. "I want to enjoy myself as much as possible."

She was honored with an Emmy for the best performance by an actress in a TV movie, although she had died before it was announced. Leonard also was nominated as best supporting actor, his fourth nomination, but the competition included John

Gielgud, Derek Jacobi, and the winner, Laurence Olivier, for his work in *Brideshead Revisited.*

Following the success of both the first and then second *Star Trek* feature films, Leonard was ambivalent about making a third film. I think we both were. We had done this, then done it again and then again, and for an actor, it was no longer challenging. Spock had died in the *Wrath of Khan,* but enough seeds had been planted in his death scene to make his cinematic resurrection viable. Trying to find that challenge that makes familiar material exciting, Leonard came up with an interesting idea: he told the studio he wanted to direct the film. That was a huge leap; he had never directed a movie, much less a movie with a substantial budget.

He was taking a gamble. When you make a demand like that, you're taking a big risk, especially in a situation where they had already killed off his character. But they also knew the value Mr. Spock brought to the story and were convinced that Leonard was serious about it. Well, he was. The studio agreed to it.

I was thrilled. Years earlier, Leonard and I had added a "most favored nations" clause to our contracts that said, essentially, that whatever one of us got, the other one had to be treated to equally. I have no memory of negotiating that. I just woke up one day, and we had a favored nations clause. That meant if Leonard got to direct a film, I would get to direct the next one. Until then, this clause had worked mostly in Leonard's favor. Each time my agents had gotten me a raise, he would automatically get the same raise. We used to laugh about it; I'd tell him that he didn't even need an agent, that he could save the 10 percent by firing his agent and just relying on mine to get us the best possible deal. But this really paid off for me; the money that my agent had gotten for us over the years was nothing compared to being given the opportunity to direct a feature.

Directing a major movie is a universal dream. There is a wonderful, and clearly invented story, that after Mother Teresa had won the Nobel Prize a delegation from the United Nations visited her in her humble surroundings. A representative told her how greatly she was admired throughout the world and said, "All that you have been given you have given to others. Surely there must be something you'd like for yourself." When she asked for food for orphans, the representative told her that while that was a beautiful request, this one time they wanted to give her something for herself. So Mother Teresa thought about it and finally said in her soft voice, "Well, I have always wanted to direct."

That was every actor, ever. And now Leonard was being given that opportunity. It actually was something he'd been preparing to do for almost his entire career. Early in his career, he once said, people had been telling him he should be directing. Instead of being flattered, "I took it as an insult. I thought, what's wrong with my acting?"

Obviously, that wasn't the rationale behind that suggestion. Leonard just always came across as being smart, as being analytical. Maybe it was the cadence of his voice or the way he used the language, but he projected his natural intelligence. That's what made him a good teacher, and it probably was what people saw in him when they made that suggestion. He started learning how to direct early in his career. While in the army, he directed training films in addition to starring in and directing plays like *A Streetcar Named Desire* for the local theater company he had helped establish. Through the years, he paid attention to the way different directors worked and learned from almost every job; from the early days of TV he learned how to be economical, how to shoot fast and get what you need right away. A lot of directors protect themselves by doing several takes of the same scene, figuring at least one of them would be useable. Before videotape was available, that sometimes got to be expensive as well as time consuming. On a set, time really has a cost. Among those directors he worked for in those days was Jack Webb on *Dragnet,* who was a master at shooting quickly and cheaply. Webb used lots of close-ups. He would bring actors in, stand them up against the background, and have them say their lines directly to the camera. Often the person they supposedly were talking to wasn't even on the set. An actor might come in, read his lines, and leave without making the slightest contact with another actor. Norman Felton, the producer of *The Man from U.N.C.L.E, Dr. Kildare,* and several other shows, was known for helping young directors learn the process. Leonard spent several days on the *U.N.C.L.E.* set trailing Joe Sargent, who would later direct great feature films like *MacArthur* and *The Taking of Pelham One Two Three.*

Leonard's first opportunity came in 1972, when he was hired to direct an episode of the anthology series *Night Gallery.* It was called "Death on a Barge," and as Leonard said, "The script was poetry." He probably meant poetry written by Edgar Allan Poe. It was the story of a beautiful young vampire kept on a barge in the middle of a canal by her father. The water prevented her from leaving and, equally important, prevented other people from getting there. And then the canal was drained!

Leonard, dear Leonard, as only he could, described it as the story of "Romeo and Juliet in vampire terms."

He subsequently directed another *Night Gallery* and an episode of *Mission: Impossible,* but when he signed to do *Star Trek III,* he hadn't been behind a camera in almost a decade. I was doing the police show *T.J. Hooker* when the studio signed Leonard to direct. He had guest-starred on an earlier episode, playing my old partner who seeks revenge when his daughter is raped and there isn't enough evidence to convict the rapist. But we decided it made sense for him to direct an episode of the show. A TV cop show, a multimillion-dollar feature . . . on some level it made sense. The episode he directed was called "The Decoy," in which beautiful young Heather Locklear volunteered to be a decoy to draw out a man who is killing beautiful young blondes. The real challenge for Leonard in that script was figuring out how many different ways he could shoot Heather Locklear with as few clothes as possible. So probably it wasn't the best preparation for the movie.

Many people wondered how I would respond to being directed by Leonard. And truthfully, I was among them. The director has to be in complete charge on the set, and in our friendship, neither one of us felt we had that power. I thought it might be a little awkward at first, but I had no doubts we'd find a way of getting through it. We'd certainly had disagreements in the past and talked our way through them. Actors often disagree and have to find the comfortable middle. Leonard told a story about the first real meeting we had with producer Harve Bennett to go over the script. Just the three of us, and Harve probably thought he was the referee. Leonard remembered that I came in and said flatly, "I want nothing to do with this script."

That sounds a lot more confrontational than I remember. But without a doubt, there was some tension in the room. Perhaps even a lot of tension. The balance that we had reached in our friendship, which had worked so well, was being upset and then having to find some kind of new footing. I had some questions about the script, as most actors do, and a few suggestions. No one knew Captain Kirk better than I did, and, as Leonard always believed, I had an obligation to be kind to him. He certainly had been good to me. Leonard began the meeting by agreeing, "What's good for you, Bill, is good for *Star Trek*. My intention is to make a damn good *Star Trek* movie, and to do that, I need you to come off well." I probably didn't realize at that moment, but he already was at work as the director, providing a comforting environment for his actor. We spent the next several hours going through the script page by page; Leonard and Harve listened respectfully and agreed to most of the changes I requested. This wasn't that unusual for us; while making the first movie, we'd spent a lot of time together trying to improve that script. It was a good, long, productive discussion, and by the time we were done, I thought the script was much tighter and stronger.

The other members of the crew probably had the same trepidation I did. It wasn't easy for Leonard to step out of the group and assume command, but he successfully found a way to deal with each of them. I also think they were watching warily to see how I reacted to taking orders from him.

Early in the production, Leonard and I dealt with that. We were filming a very dramatic scene in which Kirk learned of his son's death. Leonard and I started discussing it, and we had a somewhat different approach. Finally, as we were getting to shoot it, Leonard asked everyone else to leave the set. After they were gone, we looked at each other, and, without discussing it, we knew exactly what we were going to do. I slammed my fist down on the metal console, a sharp sound that everybody heard. "Damn it, Leonard!" I shouted as loudly as I could. "I don't care what you think! That's not the way Kirk would do it! I'm not going to do it your way!"

Director Nimoy stood his ground loudly. "The hell you're not!" he yelled right back. "You're just the actor, and you're goddamn well going to do it the way I tell you! So go stand over there and shut up!"

"Oh yeah?" *Bam!* I smacked my hands together, the sound of flesh hitting flesh reverberated through the soundstage.

"Oh yeah!" Leonard raised his voice ever louder.

I was half expecting people to come running in to rip us apart, but neither one of us could hold it together any longer. One of us — I don't remember if it was me or him

— broke up, and the other one followed. Who knows if anyone even believed we actually were fighting — that line about "just the actor" probably gave it away — but they all got the point: we were the crew of the starship *Enterprise,* and we were going to have another good voyage.

Leonard handled what might have been a difficult situation very well. It helped, of course, that this was a group of talented, very professional actors. On the set, he was extremely diplomatic. After all our years together, he knew the temperament, the needs, and the size of the ego of each actor and was smart enough to understand what he could get from each of them and how far he could go to guide them. He was, as George Takei recalls, "extremely diplomatic. He worked in shorthand; his way of directing was 'a little more of that' or 'a little less.' If he thought we were going in the wrong direction, he would suggest, 'Think of such and such.' "

He actually made a point of trying to find something special for each actor. His goal, I remember he said one day, "was to find a way of putting an actor in a position to use all of his tools." One of the first days, we were shooting a scene in which Walter Koenig, our Russian navigator Ensign

Chekov, found life signs in Spock's living quarters, which had been sealed off. While I dismissed it brusquely, muttering something about the whole crew being obsessed with Spock, Chekov showed his readings to Scotty. His line was something like, "You see. I'm not crazy." Just as they were about to shoot, Leonard told Walter, "I'd like you to deliver that line in Russian." It was incredibly meaningful for Walter. His parents were Russian Jews who had emigrated from Lithuania. In the twenty years he had been playing a Russian, he'd never had a single line in that language. This was a tribute to his parents as well as his own heritage.

Steve Guttenberg remembers Leonard working very much the same way several years later when Leonard was directing him in *Three Men and a Baby*. "As a director, Leonard was always authentic, always sincere. He didn't play games with the actors. He never lied; he never said anything that wasn't true. He dealt with everybody as they needed to be dealt with, because everybody is different. And he was quite malleable, he listened, he discussed, and he let actors do their work.

"Once, I remember, we were getting ready to do a scene in which Tom Selleck and I were arguing with Ted Danson about his responsibility to keep the baby. Just before we started, Leonard passed me a folded piece of paper on which he'd written a note. 'I want you to look at this every time you start the scene,' he said. I opened it up, and it read, 'I love you.' I looked up at him and started to say something, but he put up his hand. 'Don't talk to me,' he said. 'Do the scene.'

"After we'd completed several takes, I asked him, 'Leonard, what was that?'

"He said, 'That is your subject.' It was a hugely intelligent way to direct an actor. Reading that note just before I went into the scene filled me with great warmth. It made me feel special, and I took that feeling with me into the scene. Some directors are Machiavellian manipulators; he was a Mother Teresa manipulator."

When we were working together, Leonard never gave me a lot of direction; but what he did do was put me in a position to do my best work. In a key scene in which Kirk was told his son had been killed by the Klingons, rather than suggesting a response, he told me to go with my instincts. That certainly was consistent with his belief that no one understood a character better than the actor who created it. "You have to decide how emotionally vulnerable Kirk is going to be that moment," he said. "How much of the heroic veneer you want to strip away." I didn't know for certain how Kirk would react to that news. He positioned me near the captain's chair, and as I stepped back, I simply collapsed. Leonard told me later that he thought I'd tripped. But he let me go. Then I struggled to my feet and said my line. After he cut, he came over to me and asked with concern, "Are you all right?"

"I'm fine," I told him. "Think we can use that?"

The next day, he told me that Jeff Katzenberg had called him after looking at the rushes and said, "Leonard, I just saw that scene with Bill. Why have you been wasting your time acting all these years? You're a director!" I'm not sure how much he appreciated his acting career being described as "wasting your time," but I do know how much he liked that call.

There was one scene that I thought we never got quite right. It was a light, simple scene in which Kirk was sitting with a woman and trying to keep a secret, while she was trying to tease it out of him. It was a setup that had the potential to be very funny. But I just couldn't get it. I've never seen it — I don't watch my own performances — but I remember knowing I didn't quite get what Leonard wanted. I didn't have enough spontaneity. That was a time I could have used some additional guidance, but that wasn't the way he worked. Or, perhaps, he was more satisfied with it than I was.

As a director, Leonard believed strongly that the most important element in the entire process was story, story, story. "It's always the good story," he said. "It doesn't matter how many ships you blow up, how many missiles you fire, how many fights or disasters or stunts you show. Is it a good story? Is it something you can take home with you and think about? Something that affects you or makes you feel you're part of the human race."

For art to resonate with an audience, he believed, it has to be accessible. And the best way to accomplish that is to begin by finding a personal connection to the material. So when starting a project, he would pore over the script, searching for those elements that would allow the audience to become emotionally involved. If they weren't there, he would try to find a way to make changes and include them.

When Leonard's son, Adam, decided to give up his career as an attorney and set out

255

to become a director, his father worked with him. "When I first started getting assignments, we would work together breaking down the script. He always emphasized the importance of the story over the technical aspects of filmmaking, which basically means moving the camera. 'We're just storytellers,' he said. 'We just happen to be telling these stories on film.' While in his experience he'd found that most young directors are obsessed with the camera, 'it's always about the story. The object is to do it well, and the performances, the technical problems, will take care of themselves.' We would go through it scene by scene, and I learned very quickly about figuring out the theme, the character arc, and most important, the meaning of the story, how to find my personal connection to that story."

The commercial and critical success of *Star Trek III: The Search for Spock* marked the beginning of the next phase of Leonard's career. Contractually, I was entitled to direct the next film, but my contractual obligation to *T.J. Hooker* made that impossible, so the studio hired Leonard to direct *Star Trek IV: The Voyage Home.* In this script, we went back in time to San Francisco in the 1980s. While there had always been an undertone of humor in our scripts, we never really had gone for comedy. This was essentially a whale-out-of-time story — our mission was to capture two whales and bring them back to the future — and putting the ever-logical Spock in what was then the current time offered the irresistible potential for fun. At one point, for example, Kirk's love interest asked Spock, "Are you sure you won't change your mind?"

After considering that, he asked, "Is there something wrong with the one I have?"

Leonard's handling of the clever dialogue and humorous scenes led to producers Jeffrey Katzenberg and Michael Eisner, who had moved from Paramount to Disney, asking him to direct the American remake of a French comedy that was being called *Three Men and a Baby.* The woman who had directed the French film initially had been hired to do the American version. She wanted to do a line-for-line translation, which wouldn't work for American audiences. The film was already in preproduction, and they needed a new director. Leonard stepped in and reworked the script. Just as with *Star Trek,* there were some actors who wondered if he was the right choice. Tom Selleck remembers thinking, "Well, there's a good choice. You got a guy with no emotion who's going to direct a comedy."

But Leonard's professionalism and talent quickly won the respect of the cast. Years later, Selleck said, "Leonard was irreplaceable."

That's exactly right: Leonard was irreplaceable.

As far as I know, this film was the first time Leonard had directed a five-month-old. Actually, twin five-month-olds. There were some "creative differences." There are some actors who can cry on cue; Leonard needed the baby to pee on cue. Obviously, that was going to be a problem, so they attached a tube to the baby that would produce the . . . the illusion. But when they filmed the scene, the device failed — but the baby worked. It was amazing; the baby peed on cue.

Thrilled by that, Leonard looked at the baby's mother standing nearby and told her, "That's what good actresses do!"

*Three Men and a Baby* was a huge hit, outperforming films like *Fatal Attraction, Beverly Hills Cop II,* and *Good Morning, Vietnam* to become the top-grossing film of the year with a total of $168 million. *Star Trek IV* had been the most successful film in the series, earning $109 million domestically and making Leonard one of the very few directors in the business at that time to have made two films that grossed more than $100 million.

Leonard never changed. While I'm certain the starving actor part of his personality was thrilled at the commercial success of those films, this is a business that judges talent by those numbers, and I'm certain that he was happy that other people finally were recognizing his artistic talents. Content isn't the word; I'm not sure that Leonard ever was content with his career. He never stopped reaching, but I know he took great satisfaction in that recognition.

Obviously, a lot of people were surprised that Leonard Nimoy had directed this sweet comedy that had earned a small fortune for the studio. But some things really never change. When people learned about it, there was an almost universal response: I didn't know Spock had become a director!

# ELEVEN

While Leonard and I had been bound together by circumstance, by the time we were making the *Star Trek* movies, our professional relationship had become a close friendship. For a time, it had been the two of us — and to a lesser extent the rest of the cast, against the studio — and following that, it was simply two men of almost exactly the same age and background enjoying each other's company. But it became something far more, something much deeper, when I fell in love with a beautiful young woman named Nerine Kidd.

Nerine was an alcoholic. More than anyone I knew, Leonard understood what that meant.

Something else Leonard and I shared beyond our careers was failed marriages. Of course, I beat him there; I had more than he did. He and Sandi had been married thirty-three years when he decided right around the time we were making *Star Trek IV* that the marriage had stopping working. There are always reasons when a relationship stops working — people change, the world changes, no one outside of it really knows what happens. "I don't know why I had stayed in that marriage so long," he once told me. "It was traditional, I guess. That's what you did at that time. But it was not a happy ending." Later he added, "It had to do with taking my own territory . . . I should not have been performing duties, fulfilling empty contracts for the sake of not making waves."

But he'd met a wonderful woman, Susan Bay, had fallen in love, and, on New Year's Day 1989, married her. She had come along at a good time in his life. Through the years, I got to know Susan quite well. She was a very beautiful, very capable woman. She organized things, whether it was a marriage, a party, or a career. She was a superb cook, a gracious hostess, a wonderful partner to him, and maybe most important, she made us laugh. Susan was his equal in everything, his intellect and his passions. She brought a great love to Leonard, the kind of love, loyalty, and support that every man dreams of finding one day.

It's sometimes difficult for men to retain a

close friendship when women enter their lives. There are women who become competitive and push friends away. But in this case it didn't happen. Susan became my friend too, and I also adored her. We did not live far apart, and my second wife, Marcy, and I had many dinners at their home. Sometimes we ordered in, sometimes they cooked, but we would sit in the kitchen and eat. There was a lot of love attached to those dinners.

My own marriage lasted seventeen years, although it was over earlier. "Life took us apart," she once told a reporter. "It was time to move on." When my marriage to Marcy ended, Leonard and Susan continued to welcome me into their home and, at first, shared my happiness when I told them about this wonderful woman I'd met named Nerine. Like many alcoholics — like Leonard, in fact — she was practiced at hiding it well. At times, I would see she was drinking too much and worry about it, but there always was an excuse, and I was more than willing to accept it. I knew almost nothing about alcoholism. I'd played a drunk in several shows and TV movies, but I had absolutely no concept of what it meant to be an alcoholic. None at all.

One night, though, Nerine and I had been

at a dinner party with Leonard and Susan, and she was, as Leonard described it when he called me the next day, "erratic in her behavior." That was a nice way of describing it. While those times she drank too much were happening more frequently, I was in complete denial. I loved her. If she had a problem, I would fix it. True love is stronger than a few drinks. Right?

"Bill," he continued, "you know she's an alcoholic."

"Yes," I said, but I didn't, not in the sense that he meant. "But I love her."

He was blunt. "Then you're in for a rough ride."

Leonard valued our friendship enough to be there when I needed him without trying to lecture me. In situations like that, it often is the messenger that suffers the consequences. I continued to deal with Nerine's drinking, even as it got worse, convincing myself that she, that we, could find a way to change reality. Leonard had done it; he was quite open about his appreciation for AA. He helped as much as it was possible without intruding. He would sit with her and talk about it, just the two of them, two alcoholics discussing their addiction. He took her to Alcoholics Anonymous meetings and sat by her side in what I know was a very difficult situation for her. Finally, against all the evidence, I decided that the way to cure Nerine was to marry her. Marriage would provide the security she needed; it would prove she was loved and didn't need the crutch of alcohol.

Yeah, I did believe that.

Leonard continued to be supportive. Although we had grown close through the years, the intimacy of sharing this problem brought us even closer. Both of us knew how to walk that tightrope between our personal lives and our careers, knowing how strongly each of them might impact the other. Leonard was among the few people outside my children that I could really trust with this truth. And he respected that in every way. We would talk too, and while he never tried to talk me out of the relationship, he wanted me to see clearly what I was getting into by marrying her. I appreciated his efforts — that's what friends do when they think someone they care about it making a terrible mistake — but I paid little attention to him. Instead, I asked him to be my best man at our wedding. While certainly he must have known how little chance there was that this would work out, he agreed. Nerine and I set a date and planned to start our life together.

And shortly before that day, she was arrested for drunk driving — with my daughter in the car. The wedding was canceled, then it was just postponed, then we set a date six months in the future. And once again, several weeks before that day, she was arrested again for driving drunk. When I told her I couldn't marry her as long as she was drinking, her response was, "Don't do this to me, Bill."

Don't do this to me, Bill. And I accepted that guilt. I spent years asking myself why. The answer, of course, is that there is no good answer. We each stumble through life doing the best we can. I loved Nerine. I was as addicted to her as Leonard once was to alcohol and cigarettes, and as she too was addicted to alcohol. But he was my friend, so when I married Nerine in Pasadena, he stood tall for me, dressed impeccably as always in a tuxedo, as my best man.

When it fell apart, as Leonard undoubtedly knew it would, he was there to support me. Nerine's drinking escalated. I tried everything; I tried rehab, I tried threatening a divorce, I tried to love her more intensely; but the monster had her in its grip and would not let go. I came home one night and found her lifeless body in the deep end of the swimming pool.

At times of tragedy, people instinctively turn to family and friends for support. And I got it. I got it from my children and from the people around me, especially Leonard. He enveloped me in his arms as his brother, and we cried together. He was always there, kind and loving and available. He tried to help me answer those questions that plagued me: What could I have done differently? How could I have changed the outcome? Why couldn't I save her?

The answer I got from Leonard was that there was no easy answer; as much as I wanted things to be different, there was little I could have done about it. There is only one person who can reach an addict, he told me over and over, and that is that addict. Until, and unless, the addict reaches the point, as Leonard did, that he or she wants to take control of his or her life, there is little anybody else can do.

Friendships are not made at times like that, but they are tested. More than ever before, I had looked to Leonard. We had already been through so many wonderful experiences together, and now we had been through a true tragedy.

Unfortunately, this was not unique for him. He had been dealing with a similar situation in his own family, a situation that fortunately reached a much better conclusion. As his son, Adam, has admitted and written about in his own compelling memoir, *My Incredibly Wonderful Miserable Life,* for thirty years he was addicted to alcohol and marijuana. His addiction was so strong it cost him his marriage and, for many years, his relationship with his father. It's impossible to write about Leonard without this being part of the story.

I can't imagine how difficult it is being the child of an actor, much less a celebrated actor. Acting is a career defined by both emotional and professional insecurity. As an actor, you live with the never-ending quest for the next role, and when you finally get that role, you live with the fear you're not good enough in it. That takes a great toll on family life. A question that never goes away, even after you've enjoyed tremendous success, is, how am I going to pay the rent next month? And even that eventually becomes, how am I going to pay the rent next year? That insecurity can be expressed in many ways, but it impacts your family. Adam once said that when Leonard first started going to state fairs, for example, long before the conventions were organized and run so professionally, he would come home with an envelope full of cash. "He loved that,"

Adam told me. "Big fat envelopes filled with cash. It was what he always called 'an income stream.' He was very big on these income streams. That cash meant a lot to him. Before *Star Trek,* he had lived with a real sense of desperation to succeed and survive."

I have lived with those insecurities my whole life. Success doesn't make them go away. Early in your career, they shape your thinking, and it doesn't change very much. The second reality of the profession that impacts raising a family is simply the amount of time it becomes necessary to spend working. The hours spent on the set are very long, and then you have to go home and learn lines for the next day. There isn't much downtime to enjoy with your family. You feel fortunate to have the work and determined to give a performance so wonderful it will lead to the next job.

And finally there are the pressures of celebrity. It can be great fun being famous. Fame offers all kinds of advantages and opportunities that are unique and enjoyable. But there also is that dark side celebrities perhaps too often complain about. It's part of the deal. When you are out in public, the public believes you belong to them. And often, as in Leonard's case, it wasn't Leonard fans wanted to meet; it was Mr. Spock. Some fans of *Star Trek,* some Trekkies, believed that we have all shared a wonderful adventure and want nothing more than to talk about it — sometimes episode by episode. Or they want to demonstrate their own mastery of the Vulcan salute. The result is that Leonard was always being pulled away from his family. There was no such thing as a simple dinner in a restaurant. As a result, Adam says, growing up, he and his father were not as close as he would have liked. And, as he adds, Leonard's alcoholism certainly didn't help. And even more than that, children of celebrities can have a really difficult time establishing their own identities. They grow up being so-and-so's son or daughter, they get used to people trying to get to their father or mother through them, or talking about them, and they know people are always wondering how big a role their parent played in whatever success they enjoy. Rather than being known and judged as Adam Nimoy, for example, he never escaped being Leonard Nimoy's son. I think Adam defined that well when he wrote, "The crowd started to grow until kids and their parents were swarming around him and I was being pushed away . . . There I was, standing in the shadows, watching this from outside, out in the dark." The range of emotions that raises is really difficult for a young person to deal with.

I was so fortunate with my own three girls. For whatever reasons, and certainly I credit their mother, they were accepting of my life and didn't let it cause damage in their own lives. It was different with Leonard, maybe because Adam was a man, I don't know, but it was different. As Adam has explained, for many years, he and Leonard had great difficulty communicating with each other. Maybe even more than the generational gap between them, the childhoods that shaped them could not have been more different. As the children of immigrants, Leonard developed a specific set of values; Adam remembers that while his family had struggled when he was younger, Spock had changed that, and as he grew up, he says, "Money just wasn't a concern for me. We always had it. I think that annoyed my father, but we had very different lifestyles growing up. He was raised in a Boston tenement neighborhood; I was raised in sunny California."

Adam started smoking pot when he was seventeen and didn't stop for almost thirty years. As a kid, he paid for it with cash he took out of those envelopes his father kept in a show closet. At some point, he began drinking too. The result was inevitable. His career and his marriage suffered and faltered. He transitioned from being an entertainment attorney to becoming a successful television director. Leonard got him his first real break. When the popular 1960s show *The Outer Limits* was revived in the 1990s, he told Adam to meet with the producers and tell them he would agree to star in a remake of an episode he'd done in 1962 if Adam directed it. That episode turned out well and enabled Adam to get an agent, and he began working regularly in television. There were nice moments like that, Adam remembered, but they were the exception.

Adam described his relationship with his father as distant for a long time. For a while, they rarely spoke to each other. "There were just a lot of conflicts, a lot of distance and resentments that we both held on to." Those conversations they did have rarely ended well. As Adam explained, "I've never had much luck arguing with him. Have you ever argued with a pop-culture icon? Have you ever argued with a guy who can cause a frenzy among thousands at a convention hall simply by performing a Vulcan hand salute?"

Later he wrote, "Sometimes I would get so frustrated trying to get through to him, trying to explain that I'm not built like him." When Adam's eighteen-year-long marriage ended in 2004 and he moved out, leaving his kids, he didn't even bother to tell his father. Just contrast that to the fear and shame Leonard felt about telling his parents when his own marriage to Adam's mother ended. Times change. Finally, though, that same year, Adam decided to take control of his own life. His controlled anger had ruined his directing career. "I was not fun to be with on the set, I had a difficult time controlling my temper and attitude." He began attending twelve-step meetings.

While part of what he learned was to let go of resentments, he just couldn't do it. It was easier not to deal with them. By 2006, Leonard and Adam were barely talking. Adam would call his father on Father's Day and on his birthday, but they never saw each other.

At that time, Leonard had been sober almost a decade. Their relationship — or lack of a relationship — was painful for Leonard, as it would be for any parent. Learning about this much later, I wondered how it must have been eating at him. We never talked about it; in that way more than any other, Leonard put on his "Spock-bag," as we referred to it so many years earlier when making the original series. Everything about Leonard was slightly restrained, from the way he dressed to the sense of calm and control he conveyed. But I knew there was something wrong. It was as much a feeling as knowing the details, and I did not want to intrude.

Finally, though, Leonard did something still so much in character for him. He confronted the situation. He reached out. He sat down and wrote a long and painfully honest six-page letter to his son. Adam said, "That letter contained his list of complaints through the last twenty years. In it, he expressed his disappointment, his resentment, and his anger. It was not necessarily all about me; it was all those things he was holding on to that made him furious at me. It was really unpleasant to have to read it in print. He wasn't very sensitive. Some of it, frankly, was perfectly valid."

For Leonard, writing this letter must have been very difficult. While it listed his grievances with Adam, it must have made him at least wonder about his relationship with his own parents. And at any time of life, that never is an easy task. They had remained in

Boston while he built his life in California. He didn't see them very often. And they never really understood why he had become an actor.

But writing this letter to Adam was, in many ways, typical. Leonard was never a man to back away from a confrontation. He never sought them out, he tried to defuse them, but he did not hold his grievances inside. When he had something to say, even to people with the power to affect his career, he said it to them. But writing this letter to his son about their failed relationship must have been terribly, terribly difficult. Adam responded, he says, as he often did to that type of challenge: he didn't respond. He followed the AA guidelines as he understood them, "Don't just do something, sit there," and practiced "restraint of pen and tongue."

He resisted responding, letting his anger brew, boil, and then dissipate. He waited several months and finally decided it was something he needed to do for his own sobriety. At that time, he was writing his book and wanted some sense of clarity. As he noted, the ninth step in twelve-step program is making amends. He called Leonard and agreed that they would go through the letter point by point. They would confront their broken relationship. This might well have been the first time in their adult lives both of them were sober. For an actor, a writer, or a director, it was a situation ripe for the stage. For a father, and for a son, it was an emotional summit. As they went through the letter, Adam wrote, he apologized for those things he had done wrong, for all the times he'd hurt his father. It bothered him that Leonard did not apologize. When they were done, Adam asked his father if there was anything he could do for him as a way of making amends. "He gave me a puzzled look," Adam remembered, "and he told me he had everything, that he was very happy with his life, that he had made it financially when he was in his thirties, and that his second marriage saved his life. He repeated that he was very happy with his life."

That meeting marked the beginning of a new relationship between them. In fact, later on, Leonard and Adam would go together to twelve-step meetings. It was, Adam recalled, a tremendous bonding experience. "He finally made himself available to me." And he perceived that this effort to be supportive was Leonard's way of making amends. At one of those meetings, they did what is known as a double-share; meaning they went to a meeting together and each spoke, one after the other, for about ten minutes, and then the rest of the group joined the conversation. Leonard had decided to change the focus of his life, placing a stronger emphasis on his family. His relationship with his son, as Leonard probably wouldn't really say, prospered. For so long, he admitted that he majored in career and minored in family, and there came a time when he decided to turn that around. I noticed that; I noticed that when we spoke, the subjects of our conversations had changed, and rather than talking about our frustration with the studio and the changing business, we would find ourselves talking about kids and our grandkids.

I don't know that any of us ever come to grips completely with the complexities of familial relationships. The entanglement of deep love, needs and desires, guilt and joy, all compressed by the pressures of the world, makes relationships with our parents and our children, our husbands and wives, very difficult to ever completely understand. I know Leonard never felt contented about his relationship with his parents. I think he tried very hard to understand them, perhaps as a means to figure out himself. He made a very meaningful trip in 1988. He always had been intrigued with the idea of tracing his own roots, discovering his own Jewish heritage. In the early 1970s, while he was directing his vampire episode for *Night Gallery,* Henry Kissinger had visited the set with his son, who desperately wanted to meet Spock and get his autograph, and the Soviet Union's ambassador to the United States, the powerful Anatoly Dobrynin. Making conversation, Leonard told the ambassador that his parents had emigrated from Russia. Dobrynin suggested he come to the Soviet Union with his parents.

Leonard liked to describe his parents' reaction when he told them about it. They were horrified; they thought he was crazy. Both of them had risked their lives sneaking out of the country; they had absolutely no desire to go back. "They thought they'd get caught and thrown in jail," he said. There was nothing for them to visit: their village in Ukraine had been occupied by the Germans during World War II, and many people they had known had been killed. They waved their hands at him. *Forget it; we're not going.*

But after we'd made *Star Trek IV: The Voyage Home,* in which we had saved the humpback whales for the future, the World Wildlife Fund invited him to Moscow to celebrate the fact that the Russians had declared a moratorium on whale hunting. While it was still the Communist USSR, the Soviet Union, our Cold War enemy, relations were warming. Leonard agreed to go — on the condition that he be permitted to visit the Ukrainian village from which his parents had come.

His parents had saved a single letter from distant relatives still living in that area. That was their connection to their childhoods. The International Red Cross was able to find members of the Nimoy family living in the city of Khmelnytskyi, about a two-hour drive from Zaslav, his parents' village. Literally hours after he had completed shooting *Three Men and a Baby,* he and Susan were on a plane flying back into his heritage. They spent several days in Moscow, where *Star Trek IV* was screened three times. During this period, there was tremendous competition between our countries, and the Russians were well known for claiming they had invented . . . well, pretty much everything. It was considered a matter of personal pride. So Leonard wasn't really surprised that after the film had been screened at the Russian director's union, he was told, "Very nice, but is not your story. It was told by great director Boris Thomashefsky in 1970. A very wonderful film called *The Whales of the Red Tide."* Leonard smiled politely, perhaps wondering if next the Russians would claim to have invented Comrade Spock.

Eventually, they traveled across Ukraine by train to Khmelnytskyi, arriving late at night. The train platform was completely deserted. They stood there, waiting. Finally, a tour guide arrived and took them to their hotel. Early the next morning, someone knocked heavily on the door. A man in a suit introduced himself in Yiddish, "My name is Boris Nimoy. I am your cousin." He took them to Zaslav, a small farming village with a river flowing through it. Wagons pulled by horses moved leisurely over cobblestone streets. A dozen people were waiting outside a modest home to greet them. But rather than greeting their relative from America warmly, they were polite but distant. As he learned later, they had been informed by authorities that someone important from the United States was coming to visit them. That made no sense to them, of course; why in the world would an important person from America be coming all the way to the Soviet Union to visit the Nimoys of Zaslav? They knew from long experience that any involvement with the government usually brought problems.

A modest lunch was served, with vodka. They began conversing in Yiddish. And after a few minutes one of the men handed Leonard an envelope. He immediately recognized his mother's handwriting. It contained several photographs of children, and Leonard was asked if he knew who they were. He identified his by then adult cousins. These pictures were at least twenty years old and, as he described them, "treasured objects from another world." The walls came down, and together, they grew the family tree. They told Leonard stories of his relatives — "Your grandfather was so-and-so, and he met your grandmother this way." They talked about the three-and-a-half-year German occupation, who lived and who died, who served in the Russian army. He had brought a battery-operated tape recorder and had them record messages for his parents. Then they took him to the local cemetery and showed him his maternal grandfather's tombstone. His grandfather's photograph was on his headstone, the same picture Leonard's mother kept proudly in a family album. Connections were made. I'm sure Leonard must have wondered what might have happened if his parents had not fled to America. This might have been his life. We had just made a film about traveling back in time, and this is exactly what he was doing. I imagine the distance from these cobblestoned streets to stardom in Hollywood might somehow be like the distance Kirk and Spock had traveled to save the whales.

Ironically, when Leonard and Susan returned to Paris, he learned his father was in a hospital, dying. By the time they got there, Leonard's father was on morphine, barely conscious. Leonard played one of the recorded messages for him but never knew if he heard them before he died. Several weeks later, he showed the photographs he'd taken to his mother. One of them was a lovely, pastoral picture of a horse drinking from the river. His mother looked at it and said sadly, "Oh, this used to be so beautiful. Look, look. It's not even clean anymore."

Leonard was quite taken with the reality that her memory of it was more beautiful than the obvious beauty he saw in his photograph.

All of the challenges we faced in our lives took place against the background music of *Star Trek*. The three years we had spent making the original shows had been stretched, for reasons that have long been debated, into the rest of our lives. We'd thought we were making a TV show; instead, we had flown boldly into legend. It truly was inescapable. I remember reading a story that Leonard had told to a reporter. He was stopped at a traffic light, he explained, and he took out his Motorola StarTAC cell phone, flipped it open, and made a call. As he was speaking, he glanced into the car sitting next to him and noted that the several people in that car were pointing at him and laughing. It took him a few seconds for the reason to click in: his phone was an almost exact replica of our "communicators." With that realization, he started laughing.

As I read that story, I started laughing — because I actually believed that had happened to me. In fact, I was quite sure of it. Except, maybe it hadn't. And I wouldn't have been at all surprised if Nichelle and George and the other members of our cast had told the same story. *Star Trek* had never ended for any of us. It was always there in some form, always.

# TWELVE

After the first four movies had established that the franchise would fly successfully into the next generation of viewers, the studio decided it was time to revive the series. Leonard actually was editing the fourth movie when Frank Mancuso, then running Paramount, told him they intended to produce a new series and asked if he would be interested in producing it. It was a great show of respect for Leonard's abilities, but he had no interest in doing that. At that point, he probably still believed he eventually would escape the tractor beam that held us so tightly to the franchise. Neither Leonard nor I had any great confidence that the new series, which they titled *Star Trek: The Next Generation,* would succeed. There was a bit of ego, of course; Kirk and Spock were the core of the stories, and we didn't see how it could be successful without them. Especially because, as I heard, Roddenberry had decided the series would take place a century after our voyages ended. The crew would be flying the fifth *Enterprise,* and it would take place in a world in which people have grown out of conflict. When the writers wondered how they could dramatize a world without emotional problems, he supposedly told them, "That's your problem."

As it turned out, Leonard and I were absolutely incorrect, as Patrick Stewart, who brought Captain Jean-Luc Picard to life, was happy to remind us when we would meet at the conventions. *Star Trek: The Next Generation* was quite successful without us, although because Vulcans are long-lived, Spock was able to make an appearance on that show. For those members of the staff that Roddenberry brought back, this was a very lucrative voyage. Contractual terms in the industry had changed, and this time the actors, writers, directors, and producers were entitled to residuals in perpetuity, and as I have been told, nice green envelopes from the various talent unions arrived at their homes every three months.

The critical success of the new series combined with the financial success of Leonard's movie *Star Trek IV: The Voyage Home* led to the making of my *Star Trek V* film, *The Final Frontier.* These films were mini-reunions for all of us, and certainly we enjoyed being back together. There was a great comfort level, although we also were well aware of the expectations of our Trekkie base. On the original series, it had just been a job, but because of that acclaim, it had practically become elevated to a calling. There was a sense that we weren't simply making a $30 million movie, we were adding to the legend! As director, I was given the freedom to make absolutely any movie I wanted to make; first the studio told me what movie I wanted to make, and then I made it. As long as I made it cheaply. My original concept was that the crew of the *Enterprise* meet God and the devil. Roddenberry turned that down. There is no God in the *Star Trek* universe, he explained; we didn't want to alienate anyone. We finally settled on a concept in which we are forced to confront an alien who believes he is the devil.

It still could work, I believed. As we developed the story, I would meet with Leonard to go over my concepts. And I remember excitedly explaining to him how Kirk and Spock would have to go down into hell and . . .

"Spock wouldn't do that," Leonard said.

Excuse me?

He shook his head. "No, Spock wouldn't do that." As I was beginning to discover, there were a lot of things Spock wouldn't do. How about if McCoy goes down to the depths of hell and Spock goes after him and . . . Spock wouldn't do that. Okay, Kirk and Spock fight and . . . Spock wouldn't do that.

It was a very difficult situation. Leonard was caught between our friendship and his loyalty to his character. Loyalty won. I felt sure he was coming from an honest place, but I wanted to say to him, "Why wouldn't your character do that? It's a fictional character. Why wouldn't you go to some dimension that you hadn't thought of that enriches your character?" I believed that, within certain boundaries, a character is what the writer says the character is. If the writer decided Kirk loved jelly, for example, I'd probably think, *I didn't know that,* but from that moment on, Kirk would love jelly. A character isn't carved in stone; it's flexible.

Spock wouldn't do that.

I didn't know how to deal with it. Leonard was my friend as well as an actor for whom I had great respect. How could I argue with him? On the earlier film, Nick Meyer, who had written and directed several movies with great success, had the power to correct him. "Well, your character does do that. That's your character." I didn't, and I couldn't. I wasn't a writer-slash-director, I was his peer. I had no choice but to accept it.

Between the demands of the studio, the authority of Roddenberry as protector of the canon, Leonard's Spockiness, and the limited budget I was given, the script never reached its potential. And I certainly agree with Leonard's belief that if the story isn't on the page it won't end up on the screen. On the set, we had absolutely no problems. It could have been difficult, but it wasn't. Part of the reason for that was my approach.

Leonard and I had very different directing styles; as someone who had taught acting and had worked extensively with actors, Leonard was experienced in helping actors interpret a script and bring it to life. He was vastly more equipped than I was to help an actor with the reading of a line or to suggest a gesture. Never once did I say, "Let's do it again, and you can do it better, or faster or slower." It would have been impossible for me to say that to someone like Leonard, who was so well grounded in technique. Instead, I liked to shoot the scene several times and let the actors, especially this group of actors, do those things that they were most comfortable and familiar with doing.

I believed that the nuances in a film can be expressed by the interesting use of the camera. When possible, I would locate the camera in a place that would emphasize the meaning of the line. I felt it was easier to do it that way than to get politic about the way the actor is playing the scene — especially when that actor was Leonard.

But even with all the problems, it was a very good shoot. As Leonard explained to Laurence Luckinbill, who was playing his evil half brother, Sybok, a pure Vulcan, "The difference between a Nimoy film and a Shatner film is that a Shatner film has a lot more running. Bill is a lot more physical; I'm much more cerebral — I'm happy to duck a fight scene any way I can. The way I approached them in the series was, when there was a way to let Bill do it, I'd let Bill do it!" Admittedly, I had always envied Leonard's genius in figuring out a method that had made his work considerably easier. It seemed like in every show I'd find myself rolling around the floor, diving, jumping, falling — and being continually battered and bruised, while Leonard just pinched his fingers together. It was remarkable he never strained his fingers.

And he was not shy about pointing that out. I think because he and I got along so well, the camaraderie on the set was quite good. We often slipped into our usual mode, which Luckinbill described, maybe accurately, as "typical Hardy Boys." We would compete about everything — who had lost more weight, who was the better athlete, and whose movie was more successful. It was a shame that in those days I didn't have the magic word to shut down all discussion about movie grosses: "Priceline, Leonard, Priceline."

While we were constrained by budgetary limitations — I especially remember the rubber rocks we had to use that, unfortunately, were so light that when they supposedly were falling from a mountain they instead bounced high into the air and almost floated down — everybody pitched in to help. All the lessons we had all learned in the early days of TV had to be applied. We were out in the desert late one afternoon; we hadn't finished the shot, and we were losing the sun. I literally stood up on a box and exhorted the cast, including an army of extras, to run to the next set. "I know you're tired," I yelled, "but you're in the army now! Let's go!" And we all raced to the next set and got it done.

Critical reaction to the film could accurately be described as critical. It proved impossible to overcome compromises I'd accepted in the story combined with the small budget we had to work with, and the film failed. It was a financial disappointment, and there were fears that this would be the last film made by the original cast. But we rapidly were approaching the twenty-fifth anniversary of our debut, and the studio decided to make one final film with the original cast. Leonard was hired to be executive producer. Because *The Final Frontier* had not performed well at the box office, Leonard, Dee Kelley, and I had to agree to accept a significant reduction in our salaries. Creating the story was where all the parts of Leonard came together so beautifully. A few years earlier, a script had been written for a prequel that began in Starfleet Academy when Kirk and Spock first met. It was a way to ease other actors into our characters. Eventually, it had been shelved, but the story itself was rewritten for the original cast. While Leonard and Roddenberry's relationship had never really gotten any better, Leonard wanted the original cast's last movie to be true to Roddenberry's original concept of what *Star*

*Trek* at its best would be: a show that highlighted and commented on the great moral questions then being debated — set in the twenty-third century. He had asked Nick Meyer to write the script, and together, they searched for a workable concept. At that time, the once great and monolithic Soviet Union was splintering, bursting apart, and spawning free nations. Meyer remembers a meeting at his house on Cape Cod; as they walked along the beach discussing ideas, Leonard suggested, "[What if] the wall comes down in outer space? You know, the Klingons have always been our stand-ins for the Russians . . ." The "wall" specifically meaning the Berlin Wall, which had just come down, but actually the Iron Curtain, which had been the metaphorical border between democracy and communism since the end of World War II. The events of that time, which obviously excited him, made the perfect background for the movie, in which the Federation and the Klingons would meet to forge a peace.

Meyer recalled that he replied, "Oh, wait a minute! Okay, we start with an intergalactic Chernobyl! Big explosion! We got no more Klingon Empire!" The Klingon leader, Gorkon, was based on Gorbachev — and it was not a stretch to believe that Klingon militants would assassinate him, as had happened to Egypt's Sadat after he signed a peace treaty with Israel.

Meyer very quickly wrote the script. In his original opening, which the studio rejected because it would cost too much to film, we saw what had happened to each of the key crew members in retirement. Spock, perfectly fittingly for Leonard, was starring as Polonius in the all-Vulcan dispassionate version of Hamlet.

This was our last time together as a cast. I don't remember a lot of nostalgia, but there was a sense of great pride in what we had created. One thing I do remember is a banquet scene we filmed that seemed to take weeks, but actually only took several days. To make the food look fit for an alien, it was colored an especially unappetizing blue. If you have wondered why there are no great blue foods, looking at our plates answered that question. The fact that these meals had to sit under the hot lights for long periods of time did not make them more appealing. The food became a great joke for the cast and crew. It got so bad, in fact, that Nick Meyer ended up offering a crisp twenty-dollar bill to any cast member who would be filmed eating the stuff. Being paid to eat is the perfect bribe for the starving actor that lived inside all of us — well, at least lived inside me. As the captain, I felt it was my duty to collect that offer. I gained recognition as the only actor willing to eat the purple squid.

*Star Trek VI: The Undiscovered Country,* our last film together, was a substantial hit, grossing just under $100 million.

While I made a brief appearance in *Star Trek: Generations,* the seventh film in the series, Leonard did not. Asked about that, he responded, "I think that *Star Trek* was kind of done with me for a while. I acted in the first six films. I directed two of them. I wrote story for two of them. I produced one of them. I was very, very active in the first six films. When the seventh film came along, there was no role for Spock. And they killed Kirk. So one would have to ask the makers of those films, and the next few, why I was not involved. I was never offered anything that was like a Spock role. I was asked to direct the seventh film. I didn't think much of the script, and I passed."

But while the five-year voyage of the *Enterprise* had lasted twenty-five years, Spock was still not ready to lay down his ears. In addition to the series and the movies, we had done the voiceovers for twenty-two episodes in the animated series. Leonard liked to joke that this was the only time in his career that he "mailed in" his performance. In show-business terms, "mailing in" a performance means to give less than a complete effort, to just sort of go through it without any real commitment. I can say without any doubt that neither Leonard nor I had ever figuratively mailed in a performance. However, in this case, we literally mailed it in. Leonard was touring with several stage shows, and I was doing my usual thirty-four projects, but wherever we happened to be they would send us a script, and we would find a recording studio and read our lines. This was long before e-mailing was possible, so we would make the recording and mail it to Filmation, which is how we literally mailed it in. Once, though, Filmation sent a crew to record me. When Leonard heard about that, he was curious why I'd gotten that special treatment. I explained to him there were three possible reasons: one, they liked me better; two, my performance was so lacking in the depth they needed to honestly convey my animated emotions, meaning I wasn't animated enough for animation; or three, they had a time problem, so they couldn't wait even an extra day. I let him decide which one it was.

When *The Next Generation* became a hit, there were occasional and halfhearted requests that we appear in an episode. There just didn't seem to be any reason to do it, and they never made a reasonable offer. Hey, Kirk had to earn a living, you know. But Leonard finally agreed to appear in a two-part episode of *The Next Generation*, mostly to publicize the then about-to-be-released feature *The Undiscovered Country*. In that episode, Spock was treated in the future with the same kind of reverence Leonard was receiving in this world for creating him. Both of them had become beloved characters, albeit only one of them was . . . was . . . well, they both certainly existed, just on very different planes. The story began when Captain Picard and Data feared that Federation Ambassador Spock had defected to the Romulan Empire, but as it turns out, he actually had chosen to risk his life trying to forge a peace agreement between the Romulans and the Vulcans. "Unification," as that two-parter was titled, drew one of the largest audiences in the seven years of voyages of *The Next Generation*.

While Leonard and I aged and prospered, *Star Trek* continued into even another new generation, until it came time for other actors to finally play our roles. To create a role that has become so iconic other actors can inhabit that space is a tremendous compliment, although sometimes it doesn't feel that way. Sometimes it feels like they just don't want you anymore. Both Leonard and I had believed for quite some time that we had been "marginalized"; that was the word he used, but it spoke for both of us. We both had accepted the reality that we were done forever with *Star Trek* when he was approached by J. J. Abrams to once again become Spock for a new approach to the material, *Star Trek* (2009). This wasn't something Leonard and I ever discussed, nor was there a reason we should have.

*Star Trek* remained a potentially very valuable brand that was not being exploited. After the new film was announced, Leonard and I were asked during a joint interview how we felt about that. We laughed, we laughed really hard, and Leonard replied for us, "So you want Paramount to say, 'We've made enough money. We're going to stop making money now . . . It's been a wonderful ride. We're going on vacation . . . We don't want to make any more money.' " We laughed a little harder at that concept.

When asked how we felt about other actors playing Kirk and Spock, Leonard was quite generous, saying, "I think they should," while I replied, "I, on the other hand, resent them totally."

Which of course was not true. Totally? Never.

This story was about the first voyage of the *Enterprise,* crewed by younger versions of all of our characters. While I have been told there was a scene written for me that had been dropped, Leonard's Spock, known as Spock Prime, did appear to seemingly anoint actor Zachary Quinto as his replacement.

Leonard agreed to do it, he said, because it was the first time a respected filmmaker had said to him, "We cannot make this film without you, and we won't do it without you."

He admitted, "I was very touched by the intensity of their feelings about the classic *Star Trek* material that we did. It felt good. It felt good. It felt like being appreciated. It reawakened something in me. It put me back in touch with something I cared about. This was a very emotional experience for me. Watching this film stirred up a lot of feelings." In fact, he admitted, watching this film, "I cried a lot. I did. I sat there and cried a lot watching it."

He did, however, made one contract

demand. He was quite firm about it. When he arrived at the studio, there had to be a pint of Häagen-Dazs coffee ice cream in his dressing room.

For Leonard, perhaps more than any other time in his career, after all those years, his own life and Spock's life came together. As he said, "I found myself extremely comfortable doing it. I found myself very close to the character. I think that in a fun kind of way, in a wonderful kind of way, my own life has come to a point where I feel more — probably as Spock would at that point in his life — comfortable in his own shoes. The Spock that we've showed all through the years always had some kind of turmoil going, there was always some inner conflict. I think I have arrived in my own life as Spock [has in his life] with more of a serenity, and I felt very comfortable playing that."

Spock's appearance in the film was a well-kept secret. In fact, in several interviews, Leonard denied the rumors that he was going to be in the film. When asked by reporters after the movie opened how he managed to keep that secret, he admitted, "Did I say I wasn't in it? Maybe I was confused. Of course, speaking, if you'll pardon me, logically, I wouldn't know if I was in the movie until I saw the movie."

I had quite a different response to the movie in which I did not appear. I took J. J. Abrams out for the very best sushi he has ever eaten, which I know is something he will never forget. And if he should, I will remind him. I have great respect for J. J. Abrams. He is an extraordinarily talented filmmaker. The fact is there are all kinds of emotions entangled in *Star Trek* for all of us, and J. J. was placed in a difficult position of being respectful to the roots while growing a $140 million tree.

It is possible I felt a bit slighted. Just after the film was announced, Leonard and I were together at Comic-Con in San Diego. We were talking about the film, and I happened to mention, just happened to mention, that I hadn't been asked to be in the film. Finally, Leonard said, "Bill. Bill."

"What?"

"Do you remember *Star Trek: Generations*?"

Admittedly, it all fades together for me. "No," I said. "Which one was that?"

He smiled. "The one you were in and I wasn't." Ohhhh.

Leonard actually was given the right to approve the actor cast in the role of young Spock, Zachary Quinto. While preparing for the film, he got to know Quinto well;

Quinto was in an even more difficult situation than Abrams, knowing he would be measured against a legendary character. In this situation, Leonard's generosity to another actor was really noteworthy. Rather than being protective of his creation, he offered Quinto friendship, guidance, and praise. Whatever his feelings about Spock, Leonard's support for another actor gave Quinto the freedom to do his own best work. Rather than imitating Leonard's Spock, with Leonard's complete permission, he reinterpreted the character. As Quinto told *Time* magazine, "Initially, I was coming at it all from a strictly creative standpoint. I wanted to know that I had his support and that I could utilize him as a resource and guide through the journey of discovering who this character is for me. But what I never imagined was how close we would become, and what a father figure he would be to me."

They had one scene together, a scene that Leonard described almost as a father talking to his son. But the real purpose of the scene was to allow Leonard to give his approval to his successor. "We bookend the Spock character," he explained to *LA Times* reporter Geoff Boucher. "He's playing a Spock still looking for a balance between logic and his emotion and my Spock, well, he's gone through many years of life and arrived at a condition very much like the position I am here in my own life. I'm very comfortable with my life, my choices and my instincts. I was pretty much playing who I am today. I didn't have to search very hard to find the character I play in this movie. And I think that was the end."

Pure Leonard, of course. After all those years, still exploring his character. And it wasn't exactly the end of it. Leonard made a cameo appearance as Spock in the 2013 film, *Star Trek Into Darkness*. The reason he did it, he said, was that J. J. Abrams asked, "Would you come in for a couple of days and do me a favor." It was that simple. But personally I suspect he just couldn't resist visiting with a dear friend that one last time.

It was the last film he made.

In addition to our friendship, our memories, and the financial security, Leonard and I took one more thing with us from *Star Trek*. We were making an episode entitled "Arena" in which Kirk had to fight to the death a monstrously strong reptilian known as Gorn. Early in the episode, they had beamed down to a planet and were attacked by the Metrons. During that attack, Spock and Kirk had to evade several explosions.

Unfortunately, they got too close to one of them. As a result, both Leonard and I had ringing in our ears, me in my left ear, Leonard in his right. Unfortunately, it never really went away. The condition is called tinnitus; it affects as many as forty million Americans, and in severe cases it can be debilitating. Although the irony that Leonard suffered an injury to his ear could not be ignored, my tinnitus was considerably worse than Leonard's. For me, the sound was like radio static playing continuously in my ear, a radio I couldn't turn off. While Leonard adjusted and his mind learned how to mostly ignore it, I searched for help. At the worst moments, I thought that I couldn't live with it. But finally I went through something known as tinnitus retraining therapy (TRT), which taught my brain to ignore the sound. Long after the series ended, though, we carried that reminder with us.

The series and movies were not the only time we worked together on film, however. The relationship between Nimoy and Shatner was almost as well known as that of Spock and Kirk. While we didn't have action figures created of the two of us, as our characters did, people understood that we had a loving but sometimes competitive relationship. "Look, everybody knows that we have become very, very good friends," Leonard said. "But we've always been like two competitive siblings." And that, of course, made a great backdrop for a series of commercials we did together for Priceline and later Volkswagen.

There were three Priceline commercials, all of them based on that competitive aspect of our friendship. The concept was a simple one, and it was explained in the first spot: Priceline had decided to replace me as its spokesperson. In this mythical spot, they told me that I was being replaced because "the new" Priceline was offering fixed low fares in addition to the established name-your-own-price opportunities. I was stunned, naturally, and asked, "Who could possibly replace me?"

Then the door opened, and Leonard walked in.

In the second spot, I came up with a great idea. He was sitting comfortably behind a large desk as I excitedly explained to him that we could each represent a segment of the company. Leonard thought about it, then said, "No."

In the third commercial, he literally closed a hotel door in my face. Good fun, it was all in good fun. I mean, certainly we were competitive, but it never leaked over into real life. I mean, a little maybe, but we both knew it was all in fun. At least I knew it was in fun.

In 2014, we worked together for the last time. We did a Volkswagen commercial — for German television. It was a simple concept to introduce its new electric car. In recognition of the international appeal of *Star Trek,* a young German boy recognizes me. As the theme plays in the background, he runs into his room, which is filled from floor to ceiling with *Star Trek* memorabilia. Then, as the *Star Trek* theme plays, a garage door slowly lifts open to reveal — the new Volkswagen — with me driving. As the two of us drive along, we suddenly stop next to a futuristic concept car — with Leonard driving. He looks at us, looks at the car, and says the one word that so defined Spock: "Fascinating."

It's hard to believe that was the last time I saw him, but it was.

# THIRTEEN

It took that terrible disease, chronic obstructive pulmonary disease, to slow him down. There is no one I've known who found it more difficult to simply do nothing than Leonard. His was a life spent in motion; his mind was always racing ahead to the next project. At the height of his fame, for example, he decided it was time to finally get a college degree. While touring the country with various shows, he earned a degree from Antioch College. "I chewed up the whole elephant," he said proudly, and he later was awarded an honorary doctorate. I mean, just think about this: his professional success was assured, he had sufficient money in the bank, he was realizing his childhood dreams by performing great theater in front of filled houses — and yet he had a need to fulfill his intellectual curiosity.

Adam Nimoy once said to me, as we

wondered about Leonard's inability to just be still, "Artists do these things because they have to; it's not even a conscious choice. They just have to stay busy and challenge themselves to create." Van Gogh averaged two paintings a week for almost a decade, Adam pointed out, which might well have been the source of Leonard's fascination with his life. "Van Gogh was so focused and driven, and my dad was that way too. Both of them had a passion to create, to express themselves through their art. That's what really turned my dad on."

For Leonard, that art was photography. In addition to the economic freedom that *Star Trek* provided, it allowed Leonard creative freedom. As he told a reporter while rehearsing for the play *Sherlock Holmes,* "I've got nothing to prove to anybody anymore." For a long time, I didn't know about his passion for photography. When we were doing the show and he initially appeared with a camera in his hand, I thought, *Oh, that's nice, Leonard is going to take some pictures.* But I didn't have the slightest idea how passionate he was about it, or that he was an artist and this was his medium. In our many conversations during those years, he rarely mentioned photography, or if he did, it was in passing, nothing more than "I just bought a new camera."

"Great. I'm looking for one too."

But he must have had this interest that I knew nothing about for a long time. My wife, Liz, and I have some wonderful art in our home, but if I had to divest myself of everything extraneous in my life, except one thing other than my house and my family, I would get rid of the art and go with my horses. For me, horses are great art, and I can participate in the creation of that artistry by raising, showing, and riding them.

Unlike me, Leonard would have sacrificed anything other than those obvious things for his art, for his photography. My relationship to photography was simple: essentially, I enjoyed looking at nice pictures. Photographs, for me, captured memories. But for Leonard, the camera was something very different. And his deep passion for that art actually surprised me over the years. Steve Guttenberg remembers walking with Leonard outside a hotel, where a group of fans were waiting patiently. As those people started taking pictures, Leonard quietly cautioned Steve, "The camera takes your soul. Be careful of that."

While Steve took it as a metaphor for the business, I suspect Leonard was stating simply the potential of a photograph to convey so much more than a captured image.

He had become fascinated by photography when he was thirteen years old, when his uncle gave him the bellows Kodak autographic camera that had been bought for him on the day he was born — a camera, by the way, that he kept for his entire life — and he learned from a young friend how to develop his own film. "I thought it was marvelous to be able to shoot a roll of film, go immediately into a darkroom — in our case, the family bathroom — develop the film, and make a print. I could buy a package of chemicals from Kodak for fifteen cents, and I loved the idea of being able to capture an image that way." It was a form that expression that obviously intrigued him his whole life. In the early 1970s, for example, he began studying photography seriously, taking classes at UCLA and, for a time, considered pursuing it rather than continuing to act.

When talking about his photography, Leonard liked to quote his instructor at UCLA, Robert Heinecken, who at that time was championing photography as an art form rather than a technique to capture an instant. The difference, Heinecken said, was how you reacted if you happened to be walking down a street with your camera in your hand and you saw someone falling through space from a tall building: if you shot pictures of it because it was an event in progress, that was photojournalism, but the artist wouldn't shoot that picture unless the theme he or she was working on had to do with the effects of space on the human figure.

Leonard got that. While for most people photography is visual, for Leonard it eventually became conceptual. "At the most primitive level . . . you've got to be able to capture something that speaks to the audience immediately. Photography works on two levels, one emotional and one technical. The emotional impact has to do with looking for something dramatic happening . . . something that reaches out and touches somebody in some way. The technical is having to do with composition and framing — light and dark, light and shadow.

"For many years I carried cameras wherever I went and photographed whatever was of interest," he explained. "That's changed. I no longer carry a camera looking for someone to take a picture of. I get an idea about a subject, then I get my cameras and explore that idea visually, to find a way to express it in photographs."

Later he added, "While in film the story can unfold, in photography the story has to be captured in total in one moment. I've learned to use cameras to explore thematic ideas."

While a lot of his work focused on the female form, in the 1980s, he did a whole series called *Hands,* a series of portraits of, obviously, hands. When you look at these black-and-white photos, some showing age, others elegance, or symbolism, it really does make you pause and think about hands. And then it brings your attention to other people's hands. After looking at his photographs, it's almost impossible not to simply look at other people's hands in a new way, with a new appreciation. Years later, his representative in the fine-arts world described his work as "very sensual. But the other thing about Leonard's work is that he is always interested in the backstory, why something was what it is." That's interesting, because as an actor, the backstory of a character is what we are always searching for and too often don't find in the script. I'm not a photo critic, I know what I like, but when I look at his pictures I find myself pausing and thinking about that backstory. Whose hands are these? What do they say about that person?

Something else Leonard and I shared was our appreciation for the female form. He had the audacity, or the talent, to photograph. I would kid him about those beautiful nude models, but he was very professional about it. He began photographing nude women early in this part of his career, but it wasn't the beauty that he was trying to capture. In fact, his models in many of those early pictures wouldn't be considered especially sensual. The way he described it is that he didn't shoot the body as an object but rather as a means to express a very specific idea. In the 1990s, he posed his both Caucasian and African American models almost as statues, using lighting to emphasize the beauty of the female form. I thought those photographs were especially beautiful, and I remember kidding him about that. It actually was this series that got me in some difficulty.

My involvement with photography started when I was approached by *Playboy* to do a guest photography shoot. They asked me to shoot a playmate. And I thought, *Wow, Leonard did that, so I should be able to do that too.* Although admittedly when I thought about doing this, I suspect my very specific idea was somewhat different from

311

Leonard's. I knew my beautiful wife, Elizabeth, would probably not appreciate the artistic elements of this, so to spare her that, I decided it would be best not to mention it. I figured, *Look, it's only* Playboy; *who's ever even going to know that I did it?*

By the end of the shoot, it was all rear ends and stomachs and heads and hands; just like Leonard, I was shooting the female form as an object. A very beautiful object. Not only was I the photographer, I also was the subject: Shatner shoots *Playboy* models. And as it turned out, I was correct; when Liz found out about it, she did not focus on the artistic merit. My whole rationale — *If Leonard can do it, why can't I?* — didn't seem to make quite as much sense in reality as it had in the decision-making period. To Liz's credit, she did not ask me, "If Leonard jumped off a bridge, would you have to jump off a bridge?" She also did not admire my photographs as much as we did Leonard's work.

In his later years, he created three major works in which he accomplished exactly what he had set out to do, use the lens to explore grand themes. For the first one, called *Shekhina,* he returned to the same subject that had led to the creation of the Vulcan salute. That day in the synagogue in which he sneaked a peek at the congregation hiding their eyes obviously had a lasting effect on him. In these photos, Leonard has photographed lovely women wearing religious items. The point of these works, he said, was to find "the feminine aspect of God." The photographs as images are striking, but they became quite controversial. They also served to renew Leonard's own connections to Judaism.

Many times on the high holidays, my wife and I would go to services with Leonard and Susan at their synagogue. The two of us would sit next to each other and pray together. I'm a spiritual person more than a religious person. I'm probably more attached to the energies of various places on earth than with the singular God who wrote the Bible. Leonard retained a much closer relationship to his roots. So on the high holidays, he'd tell me he'd bought tickets for us so we'd go. In some ways, I guess, it was a way of strengthening our bonds of friendship. It was a renewal, a confirmation.

But Leonard once admitted that his Judaism had "gone flat." By that, I think he meant that while he continued to follow the broad rituals, his spiritual connection had dissipated. As he explained to Nadine Epstein in the magazine *Moment* in 2004, "A lot of my Judaism had to do with going through the motions. That meant going to the service, knowing when to stand up, knowing when to sit down . . . I'd come away thinking, did I really get what I was supposed to get out of that experience? . . . The answer was not always yes. I realized that a lot of the time I was going to these services because I should."

That was Leonard, always looking for the background story. The concept of the Shechinah, which is not especially well known among American Jews, fascinated him, and this project really allowed him to explore important issues in modern Judaism — as well as forcing other Jews to respond to his photographic statement. And I guess that's as good a definition of art as any other.

The photographs were published as a beautiful book, and the mixture of religion and sexuality was predictably combustible. When the book was announced, he was invited to speak by several Jewish organizations — but then those invitations were canceled. An Orthodox rabbi in Detroit threatened the Jewish center where he was scheduled to speak that if they allowed him to do so, he would take away the center's kosher certification. When the Jewish Federation in Seattle disinvited him, a local temple asked him to speak — and about seven hundred people showed up. That's the kind of response that I absolutely know thrilled Leonard. His photographs were forcing people to react.

You have to remember, photography wasn't his hobby; it had replaced acting as his profession. His photographs were shown in galleries and sold to collectors. I bought several, and they were hanging in my home. His series that I especially responded to was called *The Full Body Project.* I suspect it would have been better for me if I had seen these images *before* I got that call from *Playboy.* This project started for Leonard at a seminar where he was showing some of his work. Afterward, a very large woman, weighing at least three hundred pounds, approached and said, "I'm a different body type, and I'm a model. Would you be interested in working with me?"

I can almost hear Leonard's mind clicking into gear. "How do I shoot her?" he wondered. "Was I going to be reportorial? Was it going to be editorial? Was it going to be an art project? How should I light her? How should I present her? Should I present her full frontal nudity? Should I present her as sculpture — which is finally what I chose to

315

do." They arranged this model in classic poses and "her body took on shapes like marble sculpture." When he included several of those photographs in an exhibition, they attracted by far the most attention. Leonard had found his theme. His original idea was to replicate famous images of fashion models instead using large women. As his point sharpened, he decided to explore the way American culture worships the thin body, especially our concepts of beauty. As he said, "I became fascinated with this idea."

Leonard had traveled light-years away from Spock.

Fortunately, he found a burlesque group in San Francisco called the Fat-Bottom Revue in which all the performers were unabashedly and proudly large women. Some of them, in fact, are obese. The woman who formed the group, a trained anthropologist named Heather MacAllister, told Leonard that whenever a fat person stepped on the stage to perform, it wasn't a joke; it was a political statement. That must have registered deeply with him and certainly was a spark that ignited his creativity. I think he set out to make that statement visually. They were delighted to pose completely nude for him, and the result is an astounding collection that almost forces people to pause and consider their own conceptions of the female form. In one classic photo, he has faithfully recreated the great Matisse painting *The Dance* using these large women.

As a reviewer commented, "With this work Leonard Nimoy has boldly gone where no photographer has ever gone before." Proving, of course, that there never was a way to escape *Star Trek*.

And maybe that's what Leonard saw when he mounted his last great project, which he called *Secret Selves*. It was based, he said, on a story he'd read about the Greek philosopher and playwright Aristophanes, who was searching for an explanation for human anxiety. He finally surmised that once humans had come into this world as double people, attached back-to-back with two heads, four arms, and four legs. Since the time the mighty Zeus had split them in half with his sword, people have felt part of themselves missing and have been searching for that lost aspect that makes them feel whole. His theme, he explained, was that "we all have aspects of ourselves that other people don't necessarily know about or see," and he wanted to provide an opportunity to finally show that person.

Admittedly, my *Playboy* photographs did

317

not have such a noble theme.

I understood the point Leonard wanted to make, but in a very modern context. I was thinking about Leonard's concept while I was having a wardrobe fitting for a show I was doing. The wardrobe lady brought a few pieces of clothing to my house, and we were testing several combinations to see what worked. As my character was supposed to be sharp and cool, she was dressing me to be sharp and cool. And as I looked in the mirror, I actually felt sharp and cool. I liked the feeling. In my life, I am not sharp and cool. No one who knows me well would use those words to describe me. But when I had dressed in this alter ego, I very much enjoyed the feeling and began wondering if we all wear the clothes that best fit who we are, or do we dress as the person we would like to be and then, in some way, become that person?

Leonard always dressed cool. He always had the right man bag, while I was always stuffing things in my pockets. I wanted to look the way he looked. For the *Secret Selves* project, Leonard invited about one hundred people living in Northampton, Massachusetts, to come to his gallery there, the R. Michelson Galleries, dressed as the person they truly believe they are on the most profound level, their secret self. Over a two-day period, Leonard photographed and interviewed ninety-five people, most of them having dressed for the occasion. He also did a fascinating video of these interviews.

His subjects ranged from the bizarre to the poignant, but each of them revealed something important of themselves to the camera. A painter who did portraits of people who had fought in wars fantasized about living a simpler life in the woods and came dressed as a tree. A woman who had lost her husband several years earlier and hadn't disrobed for anyone since wanted to feel really beautiful once more and posed nude. An art critic harbored dreams of being "a mad scientist, but not completely mad," and posed holding a "nuclear blue thing" that he'd made. An accountant whose fantasy was to be a rock star, playing in front of thousands of screaming teenaged girls stripped to his white jockey shorts and started pounding away on his guitar. A young woman who felt robbed of her childhood because her father was a traveling evangelical preacher came in wearing a homemade green hoodie with yellow dinosaur spikes down the back; for just a few moments, she wanted "to be the kid I didn't get to be."

As actors, Leonard and I had spent great portions of our careers wearing the guise of other characters, so it is endlessly fascinating looking at these photographs. As with his other work, it's impossible to look at these pictures without feeling the emotion of the subjects.

When Leonard was asked why he had been so strongly attracted to creative photography, he explained, "I wanted to learn the philosophy of vision, to open my eyes to light and shadow and texture." But his provocative photographs also were the perfect accompaniment to the written word. When he first began taking studio pictures, he wondered what would be the best format to publish them and decided to produce a book of photographs and words. But rather than explanatory prose, which would have provided information about the pictures but not about the emotion, he decided to write poetry.

His curiosity about poetry began when he was eight years old, he said. He had stopped by a fountain and read the inscription with curiosity: "Cast thy bread upon the waters for thou shalt find it after many days." Taking that literally, he tossed pieces of bread into the fountain where they were quickly gobbled by pigeons. But he came back for several days, wondering exactly how many days constituted "many" and what to expect.

I did not know those first few years we worked together that Leonard wrote poetry. Rather, I didn't know that Leonard was a poet. That was a part of his soul that I hadn't met yet. That part of the brain that I had become most familiar with was his straight-ahead intellect; he was very focused on the reality of his performance, on solving script problems and negotiating a fair deal. He lived very much in the world of traffic jams, bills to be paid at the end of the month, and the next job, always the next job. Poetry didn't seem to be part of that world; it came from a very different place, and until his first book of poetry, *You & I,* was published he had never allowed me — or, as far as I know, anyone else from the show — access to it.

I did know he had a love for the English language; that I saw from the way he worked on scripts. To the occasional dismay of our writers, he wasn't an actor who settled where he thought there was a better way of doing something or saying something. From that came Spock's precise use of the language. A lot of humor on the show came from the fact that Spock responded to the specific words that one of us used, rather than the nuance that was intended. Whatever they came from, Leonard's poems were word pictures of emotion. Just as he did with his cameras, he tried to capture feelings with his words.

I am an incurable romantic
I believe in hope, dreams and decency
I believe in love
Tenderness and kindness.
I believe in mankind

That first book was intended to be a small printing, as he called it "an exploratory lifting of the mask on his inner thoughts," but the desire at that time for all things Spock made the book far more successful. There were five printings and 50,000 hardcover books in print, and — as Leonard proudly pointed out — the first printing of the paperback was 250,000. What helped sell the book, of course, was the fact that Leonard was willing to promote it by doing bookstore signings. It may have been Leonard's poetry — but fans were getting Spock's autograph. There was one memorable evening, though, at a book signing in Oradell, New Jersey, that his competition was doing considerably better than he was. The same day he was signing, Linda Lovelace, who had become famous as the star of XXX-rated *Deep Throat,* was signing copies of her book. "I had a few people in front of me," he said, laughing, "but her line was stretching around the block." Leonard did, however, come up with a strong selling pitch; he told them that *You & I* made a wonderful gift book, then asked, "Would you give your mother Linda Lovelace's book for Christmas?"

He published seven books of his poetry over two decades, and you could draw a straight line from the first book through the final book and it would become obvious how little he changed over that period. Trying to understand poets through their poetry requires higher degrees than I have, but it is obvious reading his work that from the beginning to the end Leonard was intent on emotionally defining grand themes like love, compassion, loss, and the endless search for roots. For the man who became famous playing the ultimate dispassionate character, his poems successfully bring out the range of important emotions.

While some reviewers of Leonard's photography wrote that he had found his voice through his art, in fact he actually found his voice through his voice. Making a living as an actor is in some ways a hustle. You don't let opportunities pass by. Leonard had a melodic baritone. Close your eyes and just listen; your memory will hear him for you. That voice was an important part of his actor's instrument, and even after he had mostly stopped performing, he continued to act with his voice.

There are singers who fight their whole lives for that single break; for Leonard and me, singing success came easily. I know it was not something I had ever seriously considered, and I can't imagine Leonard harbored secret dreams about one day becoming a British singing star. I mean, the rockstar look in the '60s was the Beatles mop-top and various versions of long hair. Spock's hair was exactly the opposite, more of a scraping-brush top. While we were doing the original series, a Paramount executive told Leonard, "There's a gentleman in New York who's producing an album of music from *Star Trek*. Your picture as Spock is going to be on the cover. Would you like to be involved in the making of the album?"

That was the appeal of Spock. Put his picture on the album cover and it was going to sell — and Leonard wasn't going to earn a penny from it. He just inhabited Spock;

he didn't own his rights. Six of the twelve tracks featured on *Mr. Spock's Music from Outer Space* already had been recorded. Leonard agreed to speak-sing the remaining six — as Spock. Leonard cowrote several of the songs on the album, which include "Music to Watch Space Girls By," "Twinkle, Twinkle, Little Earth," and, of course, "Highly Illogical." One more recent Amazon 'reviewer,' while enjoying Leonard's mostly spoken-word renditions, did describe a song that appeared on several later albums called "Amphibious Assault" as something "George Patton would have written on LSD."

While Leonard took almost everything he did seriously, which was our work ethic, he did not pretend to be a classic performer, admitting, "I'm an actor who records. I'd be terribly surprised if this singing career turned into anything big. I'm not passing judgment on my capabilities, but I'm thirty-seven years old and I've been an actor for seventeen years. I'm just getting off the ground as a singer."

Dot Records promoted the album heavily. When Leonard showed up at record stores to promote it, he usually was greeted by hundreds of screaming — and record-buying — kids. Although when he appeared in Cambridge, it was his mother who showed up, telling a reporter, "He looks tired. He's such a tired boy." About an hour earlier, she'd been with him at a television appearance — and as that reporter noted, she'd brought a bowl of kreplach for him. And as for his singing career, "He did have a certain ability for public speaking. He behaves himself very nice."

*Mr. Spock's Music* was so successful that Dot, which was a division of Paramount, signed Leonard to a contract for several more albums — as himself. Several of the tracks were released as singles, and Leonard appeared on several of the most popular variety and talk shows to promote them. During his musical career he released five albums; his most successful albums were in kind of a folk-rock style. In 1997 music publishers released a compilation of both of our "biggest hits." *Spaced Out,* it was called, and one reviewer described it as including "surreal soliloquies, mad monologues and peculiar parlance!"

But the one song that has attracted the most attention and remains the . . . the highlight of his musical career, brought together two iconic worlds, *Star Trek* and *Lord of the Rings.* Talk about when worlds collide. Leonard was a big fan of *The Hob-*

*bit,* so it was not at all surprising that he decided to record "The Ballad of Bilbo Baggins." It was on his second album, and he performed it on several TV shows, including *American Bandstand* and a short-lived variety show hosted by Ricky Nelson called *Malibu U.* When asked about it, Leonard described it as a delightful kids' song but said it fell under the "be-careful-what-you-do heading, because it lasts a long time." A video of him lip-synching on the variety show has gotten more than three million hits on YouTube — and when he made a commercial with Zachary Quinto for Audi of America that was the song he was happily singing.

Without question, one of the projects that Leonard had the most fun with was called Alien Voices; the "aliens" being Leonard and John de Lancie, who created the omnipresent *Star Trek* character Q. In the early 1990s, some of Leonard's friends were doing a revival of what is arguably the greatest radio broadcast in history, Howard Koch's adaptation of *Orson Welles's War of the Worlds;* the story of the 1938 broadcast that was done so convincingly that listeners in several parts of the country actually believed the earth was being invaded by Martians. Fittingly, it was the nation's first great alien-invasion story. The revival was to be directed by John de Lancie. Leonard was asked to do the Welles role. One of the benefits of being an aging actor of some repute is you can afford to do things just for fun. Leonard and I were both brought up on radio, in which great stories come alive in your mind, colored by your own experiences. Radio dramas are a lost medium, so naturally Leonard couldn't turn it down.

Apparently, it was as much fun as it sounds like it would be. In fact, Leonard and John enjoyed it so much that they decided to form a company to record more of these classic stories as audio dramas. As John explained, "I told Leonard, 'Look, you're an alien, I'm an alien. We'll call it Alien Voices and do adaptations of classic science-fiction stories.' "

Leonard apparently got it right away, telling John, "I've been looking for something that would allow me that type of creativity."

It really was the perfect concept. As John described it, "We all love radio because sound is a pathway straight to the imagination. In an age of dazzling visual effects, the mind still has the power to conjure the best scenery, the fastest space ships, and the prettiest women." They could bring some of the greatest adventure stories ever written to life for another generation.

The first two projects, which were recorded in a studio and released as audiobooks, were Jules Verne's *Journey to the Center of the Earth* and H. G. Wells's *The Time Machine.* There was, however, an unexpected technical problem: Leonard loved chocolate. Leonard's love for sweets was well known, but especially for chocolate. Apparently, there was a large bowl of chocolate kisses in the studio, and Leonard dug into it. The sound engineer finally told John that he had to tell Leonard to stop; the chocolate was gumming up the works. Chocolate apparently sticks in your throat and slightly changes your voice. Not wanting to upset Leonard, John figured out a diplomatic solution: he suggested to Leonard, "Hey! Why don't you have a delicious apple?" Apparently, apples clear your throat.

Leonard burst out laughing and had some more chocolate. But the engineer saved the recording, devising an algorithm that successfully filtered out the chocolate. "The Leonard filter," as it became known, was employed for the next several years.

After the success of the first two productions, they decided to go a step further, producing a theatrical experience in which actors would read their roles from the script in front of a live audience. That's when I got involved. They had decided to do a stage reading of H. G. Wells's *The First Men in the Moon,* complete with an orchestra and sound effects. John approached the Syfy channel and was told, essentially, "If we can get Nimoy in any configuration, we'll do it!" The performance was taped in front of 1,700 people in the historic Variety Arts Theatre. Most of the cast had appeared in one of the many versions of *Star Trek.* I was absolutely delighted to be part of this, although I was billed as "the surprise guest." I was cast as the Grand Lunar, King of the Moon! When I walked on stage several minutes into the story, I received a very nice welcome from the audience. I took my place in front of the microphone, held up my script, and said, in a hesitant falsetto voice, "Welcome to the moon." Leonard and John had to fight to keep straight faces. As an actor, there are few things funnier than being in the midst of a performance watching your fellow actors fighting desperately to remain in character and not break out in laughter. Because once they lose it, it stays lost. They inhale, they suck their cheeks in, they use every possible strategy not to laugh. Leonard and John managed to do it. The audience, however, did not.

The concept was so appealing that Leonard and John took it to Disney with the thought of adapting *The First Men in the Moon* into a feature film. Disney loved the concept but required two changes: first, they wanted an eighteen-year-old female character added to the story. And second, they did not want to do it as a period piece. When John pointed out that it would be difficult to call a contemporary story *The First Men in the Moon,* because it was well known we have already had men on the moon, the executive thought about it for a moment and then suggested, "Well, go to Mars!"

Rather than doing H. G. Wells's *The First Men and an Eighteen-Year-Old-Girl in Mars,* Leonard and John agreed to return to their original concept. They staged Sir Arthur Conan Doyle's *The Lost World: A Halloween Trilogy* featuring stories by Poe, Kipling, and Wilde, and Wells's *The Invisible Man,* which of course was perfect for an audio production.

What appealed to Leonard about this format was the emphasis on the story. "When you go back to the roots," he explained to writer Paul Simpson in the magazine *Dreamwatch,* "you discover what these authors were really thinking about, and what the social context is of some of these projects, which perhaps has been lost over the years when people have done derivative versions."

Leonard and John also did an original script that they performed mostly at conventions. *Spock vs. Q,* in which they debated the fate of earthkind as their legendary characters, proved so popular that they did a second version. Eventually, they began receiving requests from schools and universities for copies of their scripts so they could put on their own performances. It was a perfect concept for students; it didn't require costumes or sets, and the lines didn't have to be memorized. Making it easy for kids to act obviously appealed to Leonard, and he and John created another play expressly for students, *The Wright Brothers' First Flight.* While staging that play, they created an instructional video that included "important lessons and techniques . . . including the creation of special effects, sound, and original music."

Alien Voices was a solid success, lasting four years, and the audio stories remain available.

I don't think any actor ever really retires; rather I think they remain waiting for that one part that intrigues them, or captures their imagination, or, in some cases, just pays a lot. In the later part of his life, while he was always being offered things, Leonard was able to choose to do only those things that appealed to him.

He did a lot of voiceover work, which, for an actor, is comparatively easy. Easy only in terms of the physical aspect — no makeup! I suspect that was especially appealing to him. His voice appeared in two *Transformers* films; in 1986's *The Movie,* he created the memorable character Galvatron, who blasted his fellow villain Starscream, and in 2011 he gave voice to the lunar-stranded robotic warrior Sentinel Prime in *The Dark of the Moon.* In the Hanna-Barbera daytime Emmy Award–winning version of Ray Bradbury's *The Halloween Tree,* he served as the children's guide, Mr. Moundshroud. He did voiceovers in the mostly animated 1994 film *The Pagemaster* and the 2001 animated film *Atlantis: The Lost Empire;* he also narrated the video games *Star Trek Online* and *Civilization IV* and even appeared in two episodes of *The Simpsons.* The result, he once said, was that he successfully spanned generations of fans. "It's very satisfying," he said. "Many years ago, people used to say to me, 'My kids are crazy about you!' Now I have kids saying, 'My grandparents are crazy about you!' "

He finally reprised Spock one final time in an episode of *The Big Bang Theory*. In that top-rated show, the ultimate geek comedy, Spock, as portrayed with a toy figure and Leonard's voice, visits star Jim Parsons in a dream sequence. But if there ever was a doubt of the respect Leonard earned from the great geek community, and the esteem in which he was held, it was answered forever in a 2008 episode of that show in which Parsons's Sheldon Cooper receives the greatest gift of his lifetime — an autographed cloth napkin that Leonard supposedly used to wipe his mouth at a restaurant. As the shocked and thrilled and perhaps diabolical scientist Parsons explains, "I possess the DNA of Leonard Nimoy . . . Do you know what this means? . . . I can grow my own Leonard Nimoy!"

Actually, while they were shooting that episode, Leonard was asked to sign the napkin they would use. It was kind of a gag for the cast, which he did gladly. That napkin, now framed, hangs over the main set of the show.

That voiceover was Spock's last appearance on TV, although he was always with Leonard. I remember Leonard telling me one day he'd met Barack Obama. This was sometime in 2008, just after Obama had announced his candidacy. It was not surprising that Leonard was invited to a luncheon to meet him. I suspect it pleased him a great deal, given his lifelong political activism, that a young African American would be a serious candidate for the presidency. It was a small group of people at someone's home — a typical politician's meet-and-greet and by the way do you have your checkbook with you. But as Leonard told the story, "We were standing on the back patio, waiting for him. He came in and walked through the house, and then he saw me. He stopped — and held up his hand with his fingers separated, the Vulcan gesture. And he smiled, big smile, and said, 'They told me you were here.' We had a very enjoyable conversation, and when we were done we shook hands, and I told him, 'It would be logical if you would become president.' "

He did play one final role; that of a scientist living in an alternate universe in J. J. Abrams's TV show *Fringe*. When asked why he took this role, Leonard explained, "I did not intend to do any more work. And the fact is I don't consider this work. This is great fun." The show, which ran for five seasons, is a future-fiction drama concerning the crime-solving exploits of the FBI's little-known Fringe Division. The show is a little bit of a lot of shows, everything from *The X-Files, Altered States, The Twilight Zone,* and cop procedurals like *CSI.* While Leonard's character figured prominently in the plot, he appeared only as a voice; the writers came up with clever ideas when his physical presence was necessary, including an animated episode and a storyline in which he possesses another body.

After the first two seasons, Leonard felt his character, William Bell, had become too nice a person, which left him, as an actor, no place interesting to take the character. But then the writers twisted perceptions, turning Bell into a mostly evil character — and regaining Leonard's interest enough for him to agree to make a surprise appearance on the show. "J. J. Abrams is a friend of mine," he said. "When he calls, I listen. I'm still a sucker for a good role, so it was pretty easy to convince me that there was an interesting challenge in the character. It allowed me to play aspects of a character that I haven't played in a long time." One last time, he got to play the villain.

# FOURTEEN

The details fade over time. Where we ate dinner, appearances we made together, arguments with the studio. The countless days and nights Leonard and I spent together become blurred into larger memories. When I think about Leonard, my memories are emotional more than specific. How lucky I have been to have shared this adventure with him, my "Siamese twin," my "brother from another mother," my best friend.

Between the photography and the jobs and writing poetry and working around the house and speaking engagements and appearing at the occasional convention, where the entire crew was treated like royalty, he led a full life. But his focus had changed. Like all of us do, he had made promises to himself many years earlier. "If I ever make it, if I ever make a living, if I ever become solid, I will do this and that." But like the rest of us, that place of contentment was always after the next job, after the next success. Until his disease began to slow him down, he never got there. And then, when he couldn't work as much as he wanted, when he couldn't travel as much as he wanted, he finally arrived at that lifelong destination.

He had decided to major in family, to heal whatever last rifts still existed. We talked about it, publicly, and he admitted, "We have spent the last several years consciously trying, at least I have, and I think my son and my daughter have felt the same, trying to build a new relationship."

"We learned to appreciate each other," Adam remembers. "He spent more time at home than ever before, and he would sit there and tell stories. Just about every other weekend we'd have the kind of big family dinners that we hadn't had too much in the past. There was a lot of love there that we all finally were able to express."

Unfortunately, tragedy also can often be the thing that brings people closer together. In 2008, as Adam Nimoy was putting his life back together, he met a woman he describes as "loving and joyful. A woman with no agenda." Like so many parents, Leonard and Susan wondered if Adam had become sober and put his life together because of this woman, or if he had been able to meet this woman — Martha was her name — because of the changes he was making in his life. After getting to know Martha, one night Leonard and Susan called to tell Adam how much they liked her, and how happy they were about the impact she was making on his life — especially the fact that his relationship with his father and Susan had changed so dramatically. At a different time that might have become a point of contention; Adam was proud of the hard work he'd done on his own to change his life. "But I didn't say anything about that. I simply said, 'I really appreciate the phone call, and I am really happy about my relationship with you guys too.' "

Martha did bring her joy into all their lives, and in January 2011, Adam and Martha were married. Four months later, Martha was diagnosed with terminal cancer. As Adam recalled, "When my first marriage ended in 2004 and I moved out of my house, I didn't even call my dad. When Martha was diagnosed four months after we married, the first call I made was to my father."

For the next year and a half, the whole

family fought the disease, and as Adam remembers, Leonard and Susan were there "every step of the way. We were lucky; my Directors Guild insurance paid for everything. I didn't need financial help; I needed emotional support, and I got it. Nobody kept me going more than they did. They were both physically and emotionally supportive. They brought food. They visited. They did anything and everything possible to help us. It was a complete turnaround."

Adam became Martha's caregiver. "It's an extremely difficult thing to do," he said. "You need support; you need a lot of support. I had it. Martha's mother, my sister, Julie, people at UCLA where I was teaching, and the twelve-step groups that I was part of. But the lengths my dad and Susan were willing to go to, to help me, were amazing. Through this time we formed a whole new relationship."

On December 9, 2012, Martha died. Her legacy, in some way, was to bring Leonard and Adam closer, perhaps, than they had ever been as adults.

By that time, though, Leonard's own mortality was beginning to show. It's impossible for me to remember the first time I truly understood the toll Leonard's disease was taking on him. I remember sharing a car one afternoon that was to take us to a venue where we would make another appearance together. It was something we'd done countless times, and always both of us had walked briskly wherever we were going. Get there, get it going, have fun, get it done. But this time as we walked, Leonard had to stop and lean against the wall to catch his breath. Over time, those stops became more frequent. Then there would be an oxygen tank with us in the car. His illness made him angry. He'd curse it, "Goddamn it." Then he would shake his head despairingly and ask me again and again, "Why didn't you stop me from smoking?"

I can't begin to express the feeling of helplessness I felt. This was one of the most active people I have ever known, and his world was shrinking rapidly. And there was nothing at all I could do. The very last thing Leonard wanted from me was sympathy.

For an actor, this disease is a special kind of horror. An actor's voice is his or her most important tool. It is an instrument as much as any flute or tuba. It can carry an audience from Shakespeare's London to Leonard's Vulcan. Acting begins in the lungs, where your voice is manufactured. As you breathe air out, it strums against your vocal cords to create your unique sound; if you don't have the air, there is no strumming, and you are robbed of your voice. For an actor, losing your voice means losing your career. A lot of actors take their voices for granted; it's always going to be there — until it isn't.

Richard Arnold, who spent considerable time with Leonard organizing conventions and appearances, remembers noticing the first real symptoms of Leonard's COPD as far as back as 2006. "He began having to clear his throat more often. You'd hear just a little *ahem* when he was talking, then progressively it got worse. One afternoon we were in his office while he signed memorabilia, and his voice was really rasping. I'd heard that before, but never this bad. I got worried and I asked him, 'Leonard, are you okay?'

"He smiled and reached across the desk, put his hand gently on top of mine, and said, 'Richard, I was a really good smoker.' For thirty years he had smoked two packs of cigarettes a day, and finally it was taking its toll. Over time, he became really raspy, and his breathing difficulties became more obvious. When I would see him, he had clips in his nose connecting him to an oxygen tank."

Leonard attended his last *Star Trek* convention in Chicago in October 2011. Leonard had finally accepted the fact that these trips were too difficult for him. For the first time, he brought his entire family with him; Susan, his children, grandchildren, and his one great-grandchild. He hired two shuttle buses to move them around the city. It was a very dramatic situation. Zachary Quinto had put together a video tribute in which everyone from J. J. Abrams, and several other actors from the more recent *Star Trek* films acknowledged their debt to him as well as their appreciation and admiration. As Leonard was being introduced, he stood backstage, by himself, fighting the tears. And then he walked on stage to a huge, huge standing ovation. The packed arena was telling Leonard how much he was loved; and he had the joy of knowing it.

It was not his last appearance at a convention, though. He continued to get large offers to attend one final convention. Then one more after that. Organizers were willing to pay him far more for showing up for a few hours than we had been paid for the entire three years it took to make the series. As Richard Arnold told him when relaying these offers, "This one could pay for your great-grandson's entire education."

"I know," he said, "but that's already taken

care of."

For someone like Leonard, who was never still, it must have been so difficult to turn down these offers. Not for the money — the money was wonderful — but for the chance to share with legions of fans just one more time. It isn't possible to explain what it feels like to be standing — or in our case, sitting — on that stage. Leonard knew, and I knew, and Patrick Stewart and a few other people know that feeling. But being at one of those conventions, standing in front of that audience, feeling their energy and their love, is as close to understanding "the force" as any of us will ever come.

Someone came up with the means to overcome Leonard's physical limitations; Leonard could appear at a convention being held in Florida on Skype. The promoters sent technicians to his home, and they set up the system on his desk. There was a wonderful irony to it; the kind of space-age technology that was featured in the original series but did not exist in reality was making it possible for him to talk about it. He'd have his talk, then the fans lined up in front of a computer at the site, and as they said their names, he signed a photo for each one of them. They received them the next day.

"It was terrific," Leonard said, then added,

"I didn't even have to get dressed!"

He kept telling organizers, "That's it; I'm retired," but he could never resist just one more project. Work was in his DNA. He was as addicted to creating as he once had been to cigarettes. And so he never did really, really, really fully retire. There was always just one more appearance, one more project that interested him or engaged his curiosity. Among those last projects in which was he was enthusiastically involved was a memorable trip back to Boston. As a way of thanking his father for everything he had done, Adam proposed a short documentary, and the two of them went back to Boston and filmed *Leonard Nimoy's Boston.* It started out meant to be a family album, but turned into a PBS special.

Watching Leonard's enthusiasm as he shares the stories and places of his childhood with his son made me pause and remember the Leonard I had known for so long, the young and energetic Leonard, easing into stardom. "This is where I learned to sail . . . I worked here stacking chairs . . . I passed by this church every day of my life . . . we lived on the third floor, right over Harry Rubin's Credit Union . . . There was one building, a few blocks away, that had an elevator." And then, typical Leonard, he spoke with warmth about his own parents, telling a story I had never heard, but knowing him so well a story that did not surprise me at all. One night, he and a friend had worked till close to midnight folding chairs at the band shell, and he was coming home with the two dollars he'd earned when he met his mother and father, who were worried and had come looking for him. "My mother said, 'Where have you been?' 'We were stacking chairs.' 'This late?' 'Yeah, we just finished.' I handed over the two dollars. My father grabbed it out of my hand and tore the two dollars in pieces. He was so angry because she was upset, and that upset him. He couldn't take it.

"So she picked up the torn pieces. She wasn't going to let the two dollars go. We walked home in silence."

And then, near the end of this wonderful twenty-eight-minute documentary, Leonard became a bit melancholy, remembering the West End neighborhood that had been torn down, his childhood lost to urban renewal, and he said wistfully, "I miss Boston. It was a good place to be."

The satisfaction the two men got from working together led Adam to propose another collaboration. The year 2016 marked the fiftieth anniversary of the original series, and to celebrate that, Adam suggested they make a documentary telling the story of Spock. Leonard agreed to celebrate Spock, but he was emphatic that he did not want it to be a Leonard Nimoy documentary. It was to be Spock-centric, and he would participate only to talk about all those things he brought to the creation of Spock, from his feelings of alienation in Boston to the struggles of his early career. "He wanted to do it as kind of a farewell gift to the fans that he loved, honored, and respected," Adam said. "He was very grateful to them for creating this whole fan-based phenomenon. This was going to be the definitive work on Spock. How he came into being, how he helped Roddenberry give life to the character, how the character evolved and became iconic, and what it is about the character that people have identified with and why has Spock stayed alive in the pop culture for so long.

"So we sat down and started talking about it. We were going to put it on camera; I was kind of in a hurry to film him on camera, but he thought we had plenty of time. And then he got sick . . ."

Leonard and I began talking about our own mortality several years ago. I said to him, "Perhaps the reason I'm running as fast as I can is I see very clearly my own death . . ."

"I think of it as a loss of consciousness," Leonard responded. "And I am conscious of it. I think about it . . . I think about the loss of relationships, the end of that. I think about the loss of creative opportunity; which I love to be creative, to see things evolve . . . I think it is important now to be making philanthropic statements, to be giving, giving back, giving back as much as I can, as much as we can, to the community and to various venues, funding for arts, funding for children, funding for education, things that we believe in and care about, leaving a legacy . . ."

Leaving a legacy. As you get older, if you've been fortunate enough to earn more than enough money to take care of your family, you begin to think about exactly what to do with it. It forces you to think about those things that are most important to you, the way you want people to remember you. The legacy an individual leaves is a fascinating way of looking at a life. The measure of a man, or a woman, is what is left behind to make the world a better place. So it is not at all surprising that Leonard and Susan actively funded the theater, artistic, and educational programs. This isn't the kind of stuff that Leonard talked about; when he saw a need, he got involved. I knew about very little of this until I read it in the newspapers like everyone else, but it certainly didn't surprise me. As far back as 1998, they donated $100,000 to the Museum of Contemporary Art in Los Angeles to enable the museum to buy a series of photographs. For several years, George Takei served as chairman of the board of the Japanese American National Museum, and he remembers, "Leonard and Susan stopped by our museum to see the exhibits, and he was so impressed that he made a nice contribution."

It was entirely fitting that one of Leonard's largest contributions was made to the famed Griffith Observatory in Beverly Hills. Opened in 1935, this classic art deco building has become a Los Angeles landmark and has been used in numerous movies, including *Rebel Without a Cause, Rocketeer,* and the *Terminator* films. But it had deteriorated badly. As Leonard and Susan donated a million dollars to enlarge and renovate the structure, funds that certainly had come from the *Enterprise*'s exploration of the universe, he said, just as Spock might have, "By observing the sky and pondering our place in the universe, people gain a new perspective on their daily lives. Griffith Observatory gives its visitors that opportunity." The observatory was gutted and completely rebuilt, including an entirely new lower level where the 190-seat Leonard Nimoy Event Horizon lecture hall, which is used primarily for demonstrations, lectures, and other activities, is located.

Leonard, of course, was always fascinated by what might await us outside our earthly bonds. He was convinced there are other life-forms in the universe. He didn't speculate on what they might look like or how they might respond to us or whether they had evolved beyond us or had remained primitive, but he knew they were out there. Having lived in *Star Trek*'s universe for so long, it probably would have been impossible for any of us to think we are here alone. Leonard always was interested in those things that lie beyond our knowledge and our understanding, and so it made perfect sense that he would make this donation to the observatory.

And finally, Leonard reached back to his local theater roots when he and Susan donated $1.5 million to renovate the Thalia Theater on New York's Upper West Side on Ninety-Fifth and Broadway. He had a special connection there with Isaiah Sheffer, who managed the adjoining Symphony Space. Sheffer ran a popular program known as Selected Shorts, in which he invited actors and actresses to read short stories for an audience. For more than twenty years, Leonard read a range of great short stories at Symphony Space, everything from James Thurber to Evelyn Waugh to Raymond Carver, stories that eventually were broadcast on radio and made available in podcasts. Again, it was his effort to make sure classic writing not only stayed alive; it reached a whole new audience. But the real reason he continued to do it for so long was to get together with Sheffer. Whenever they spent time with each other, they would eventually lapse into Yiddish. Sheffer, like Leonard, had been in the Yiddish theater, and he was one of the few people with whom Leonard could speak Yiddish. "He knew Schwartz," was the way he described him. It was their mutual love for that fading language that brought them together. *"Zayn oder nit zayn?",*" Leonard would tell him, *"Ot vos s'iz di frage.".*" To be or not to be, that is the question.

And then he might add the poem he remembered so often after he left home:

*Aufn Wehg Shteyt a boym. Zug ish tsu die*

*Mama, herr. Zollst mich nor nisht shteren.*
*Vill ich, mama, eints und tzei, bald a foygl*
*veren.*
On the Road There Stands a Tree, I say
to my mother, listen . . . Don't try to stop
me . . . In a moment, Mama, I'm going to
become a bird.

The Thalia had once been a popular movie house; known for showing classic American films and great foreign movies, always as part of a double feature. Fellini, Bergman, Truffaut, their films all played there. But it had closed in the 1987 and essentially had remained empty for more than a dozen years. During one of his meetings with Leonard and Susan, Sheffer mentioned that the Symphony Space was hoping to rehabilitate the Thalia. He wanted to build a new theater and make it part of a larger Symphony Space complex. Susan and Leonard volunteered to donate the money, and the 168-seat, wheelchair-accessible Leonard Nimoy Thalia now hosts a wide variety of events. It's exactly the kind of eclectic space that perfectly represents Leonard.

He left a lot behind, Leonard did, to remind us who he was and what he accomplished. In an interview in 2011, he said, "I have been through many resurrections in my career. I have died and come back. I have left and come back. I've been canceled and come back."

But all of that ended on February 27, 2015.

His disease had been creeping up on him in his last few years. He thought about his life and where he was and judged himself content. "I wake up in the morning and sometimes think, I finally got my reward for the tough times," he told me once. "I really do. I feel rewarded." Later he added, "I feel greatly blessed. These are the best times ever . . . I'm wonderfully happy."

He finally had what he had been searching for since his raucous childhood: a loving family. "My present life with my wife has turned into an experience that I never dreamed could be so fulfilling. I have two great kids, five great-grandchildren. So, I've had a pretty good ride."

And then, as we reminisced about the crew of the starship *Enterprise,* especially the wonderful DeForest Kelley, I said, "So you live and die."

"Actors up on the stage," he responded. "Let us hurt no more." And then he added, "Death is an inevitability. In the meantime, I think, I feel good about the fact that both you in your own way and I in my own way have found the energy and the lust for life each day, to do interesting and exciting, and creative, and productive and fun things to do. And a wonderful relationship."

I often think about friendship. Our friendship. All friendships. The complexities that bring two lives together sometimes briefly, sometimes for almost a lifetime. There are fleeting friendships and enduring friendships. It is such an all-encompassing word, but it doesn't sufficiently define the depth of any relationship. There are so many metaphors that might be applied, but ours covered an ocean of time, and as in any voyage, between the calm seas we encountered moments of turmoil. One of my greatest regrets is that Leonard and I were not as close as we had been during those last few years of his life. There was a small incident; I was making a film about the many captains of the *Enterprise,* and Leonard did not want to appear in it. I thought he was kidding; it was such a small thing. Just the next of so many projects we'd done together. But then a cameraman filmed him speaking at a convention without his permission, and he got angry. Essentially, he stopped speaking to me. It made no sense, and I reached out to him several times to try to heal this problem, but I never got a response. *I don't understand this,* I thought, but I just assumed that given time this rift would heal. Every friendship has its ups and downs. This was a temporary blip; our friendship was too strong to end because of something this meaningless.

It was very painful to me. As I'd never had a friend like Leonard before, I'd obviously never been in a situation like this, and I had no idea what to do about it. If I knew the reason Leonard stopped talking to me, not only would I admit it, I would have taken steps to heal those wounds. If I had done something wrong, if I had said something that was perhaps misunderstood, I would want to know it so I might make amends. But none of that took place. I have no idea what happened.

It couldn't have been that cameraman. In fact, after that appearance, we both flew back to Los Angeles on Leonard's plane, and he was his usual self. If something was wrong, then I certainly didn't sense it, nor did he say anything.

Leonard was not shy about confrontation; if something was bothering him, he addressed it. So this was bewildering to me. I tried many times to communicate with him directly; I tried to find out what the issue was through our mutual friends, but I never found the reason. I was mystified. It was baffling to me. I kept asking people, "What happened?" But no one could give me an answer. It remains a mystery to me, and it is heartbreaking, heartbreaking. It is something I will wonder about, and regret, forever.

Starting when we were doing the original show and throughout our lives, there constantly had been stories about our supposed feud, about our fighting. Except for those very first months, when I had to adjust to the fact that Leonard was getting more attention than I was, none of that was ever true. "Our sibling rivalry," as Leonard laughingly referred to it, but he was my closest friend in the world.

And then this happened. When necessary, we communicated through other people. Among them was Richard Arnold, who handled our *Star Trek* business and other things for both of us, who had been alongside both of us for so many decades, and understood the depth of our friendship. This is the way Richard describes our friendship; this is the way I remember it: "They loved each other so much," he said. "It was so obvious when we'd see them onstage; they didn't quite hold hands, but about as close as you can get to that, arms around shoulders. They spent so much time laughing that I said it was a mistake to do the photo ops with them first thing because they would do nothing but talk to each other the whole time.

"Those last years were tough because Bill still cared very much for Leonard and Leonard still cared very much for Bill. They both knew I was working with the other one too, so when I was in Bill's office he would ask about Leonard, and when I was at Leonard's house he would ask about Bill. Leonard was always curious as to what Bill was up to and was always amused by his crazy schedule, filming, making commercials and doing a new CD, going on an extended trip to wherever. Insane, just insane."

I knew he was sick, we all knew that, but until his last few days I did not know how sick he was. But when I finally found out how seriously ill he was, I sent him a last note:

My dearest Leonard,
I love you like a brother. Maybe when I first met you, in the beginning of our deep friendship, you might have irked me here or there. At least that's what I have been told, but I don't remember any irks, I just remember laughter.

I remember being in limousines with you, bending over with laughs. I remember the deep talks we had about family and friends and life in general. The stories you told about your grandfather and your father. The mind-melds and the interviews. I have had a deep love for you Leonard — for your character, your morality, your sense of justice, your artistic bent whether it's painting pictures or as an actor. It is with great gratitude to have known you all these many years. You're the friend that I have known the longest and the deepest. I have missed you terribly and have longed for those dinners we used to have.

I told you fifty years ago to give up smoking but no, you wouldn't listen. Now my advice is to relax, be happy. You're a wonderful man and I, along with so many other people, think so highly of you. Good luck my dear friend.

Love,<br>Bill

I don't know if he ever read it. I prefer to believe he did. But whether he did or not, I don't have the slightest doubt that he knew the depth of my feelings for him.

The last words he said to his fans, in the

form of a tweet to his more than one million followers, was "A life is like a garden. Perfect moments can be had, but not preserved, except in memory. LLAP."

LLAP. Live long and prosper. Spock's words. In those final days of his life, Leonard and his creation, Mr. Spock, had become virtually indistinguishable.

Rabbi John L. Rosove, Susan's first cousin, described his death: "His family had gathered around him in a ring of love. Leonard smiled, and then he was gone. It was a gentle passing, as easy as a 'hair being lifted from a cup of milk,' as the Talmud describes the moment of death."

Millions of people mourned him, knowing a good man had left this earth for another voyage. President Barack Obama issued this statement, "Long before being nerdy was cool, there was Leonard Nimoy. Leonard was a lifelong lover of the arts and humanities, a supporter of the sciences, generous with his talent and his time. And of course, Leonard was Spock. Cool, logical, big-eared and level-headed, the center of *Star Trek*'s optimistic, inclusive vision of humanity's future.

"I loved Spock."

For the president of the United States to say something like that about a kid from inner-city Boston is pretty cool, indeed.

I was in Florida, one of the major celebrity guests at a major Red Cross fund-raising dinner, when Leonard died. Rather than missing that event, which raised a great deal of money to help people in need, I decided to attend the dinner and fly back the next day, although it meant missing Leonard's funeral. The funeral was scheduled for Sunday morning. I've always been one of those people who believed in honoring people while they are alive. I have always believed that we should mourn the dead but celebrate life. I received a great deal of criticism for that decision. In fact, at the dinner, I asked the more than one thousand people there to pause and remember not just Leonard but my friend Maury Hurley, a wonderful writer and producer who also had died that week. And my daughters represented our family at the funeral.

There are times in life when being a celebrity can be painful. The fact that rather than being able to mourn the death of my dear friend in my own way, I had to deal with this controversy was one of them.

I think about Leonard. I miss him. Even when we weren't in close touch, he was always in my life. And when I think about Leonard and all the adventures we had together, I remember his own lust for life; I remember his desire to explore and experience life in all its infinite wonders. I think of his spiritual side, in which he never stopped searching for answers he knew he would never find. I think of his generosity and his commitment to fight for equal justice for everyone. I think of his never-ending passion for the arts and his quest to nurture creativity in young people. And I think of him standing in front of me, his palm held high, his fingers separated in the Vulcan salute, smiling knowingly.

Fifty years is a lifetime that passes in an instant. I can close my eyes and see him, young and handsome, tall and taciturn. He's there, in my mind; his light step, his sardonic humor, his passion for his work. I hear his voice in all its richness, infused with an endless curiosity, and the sounds of his unhappiness as well as his laughter.

I look back and the reflection I see is my own life. The young actor that I was, hard of body, sound of mind, excited about the possibilities. Fifty years ago no one, no one, could have envisioned what was about to happen to us: This miracle that is *Star Trek* and a friendship that grew from it and lasted almost half a century. The fact that my contribution to *Star Trek* is done carries with it a great sadness, but that is nothing compared to the devastation of Leonard's death before we could resolve the fraying ropes of our friendship. I am filled with sadness at the realization it will never be put back together.

There is a photograph of Leonard and myself that I especially love. In it, both of us are doubled over in laughter, and it was laughter at each other. With Leonard, you earned his laughter. We were at a convention, on a stage answering questions. There had been no preparation, our answers were spontaneous, and they were intended both to respond to the audience but also to delight each other with references to the secrets we shared. There was no filtering, no guidance, but in that photograph we so clearly had found the essence of our friendship and were mutually reveling in it. It was a moment of pure and utter enjoyment for who we were, what we had achieved together, the bond we shared — not just with each other but with the greater *Star Trek* audience — and the joy we found in each other's company.

When I think about our relationship, when I think about the fact we are celebrating the 50th anniversary of *Star Trek,* that's what I choose to remember.

Leonard had a wonderful philosophy. Steve Guttenberg told me about one night he'd had dinner with Leonard and Susan. "I was busy waxing philosophic about life when Leonard stopped me. 'You just don't understand,' Leonard said. 'The world is your oyster.' That was a long time ago, and I've never forgotten those words. I've thought about them, and what I took from that was that life is a gift, and every moment is important. That I should try to make the most of every day. Go, go and have a good time."

"Find your bliss," Leonard said, quoting Joseph Campbell. "This planet and this civilization is in need. I see it as a time of need. I spoke at Boston University's commencement a couple of years ago, and I said to give us the best of what you have, we need it. We crave it, we need what you have to offer. It's important that you focus on what you can bring to the party. The rest will take care of itself, hopefully."

In his play, *Vincent,* Leonard drew from the letters of Vincent van Gogh. There was one letter that he quoted, which seems so appropriate on so many levels: "I am a man of passions . . . I am a stranger on earth, hide not thy commandments from me. There is an old belief, and it is a good belief, that our life is a pilgrim's progress and that we are strangers on earth . . . The end of our pilgrimage is the entering in our Father's house, where are many mansions, where He has gone before us to prepare a place for us . . ."

LLAP, my friend, my dear, dear friend.

# ACKNOWLEDGMENTS

There are many people I would like to acknowledge, but this book would not exist without David Fisher, with whom I have worked before and hope to work with after (soon, David, because there isn't much time left). With a deep bow and a wave of my hand, I acknowledge my cowriter, David Fisher.

I would also like to express my appreciation to the many people who so willingly gave their time and their memories to assist me in paying tribute to Leonard, among them Richard Arnold, Joe D'Agosta, John de Lancie, Dorothy Fontana, Steve Guttenberg, Leonard Sachs, Jean-Michel Richaud, George Takei, Adam Nimoy, and the others who chose to do so without credit.

As always, I appreciate my valued assistant, Kathleen Hays, who manages to bring order to a hectic life, and my agent, Carmen Lavia.

From publisher St. Martin's Press, I would like to thank executive editor Peter Joseph, who shared his vision for this book with me, and Melanie Fried, who gets it done, whatever it is, as well as Tom Dunne, for his long and honorable career in publishing that has led to this book.

I also would like to bring the attention of readers to the Archives of American Television (ATT), for "Capturing Television History, One Voice at a Time." The AAT has very quietly gone about building the great oral history of television in existence and has made it available to both serious researchers and the rest of us fans. As someone who has both participated in the collection of that history and utilized it as a resource, I remain in awe of what they have done and continue doing and urge readers to visit their site (http://www.emmytvlegends .org)!

David Fisher would like to thank Casson Masters and Scribecorp, the best friend of every writer who needs a transcription done. And most important his beautiful, always supportive wife, Laura Stevens Fisher, who is always there, wherever *there* is, at exactly the right time (as well as their faithful dog, Willow!).

# ABOUT THE AUTHORS

**William Shatner** has worked as a musician, producer, director, and celebrity pitchman, and notably played Captain Kirk on *Star Trek* from 1966 to 1969 and in seven *Star Trek* films. He won an Emmy and a Golden Globe for his role as attorney Denny Crane on the TV drama *Boston Legal*. He lives in Los Angeles with his wife, Elizabeth.

**David Fisher** is the author of more than twenty *New York Times* bestsellers, and previously worked with William Shatner on Shatner's autobiography *Up Till Now*. He lives in New York.